HOW TO READ YOUR HOROSCOPE IN 5 EASY STEPS

Stop Reading Books (Except This One...) and Start Reading Charts

First published by O Books, 2007
O Books is an imprint of John Hunt Publishing
Ltd., The Bothy, Deershot Lodge, Park Lane,
Ropley, Hants, SO24 0BE, UK
office1@o-books.net
www.o-books.net

Distribution in:

UK and Europe
Orca Book Services
orders@orcabookservices.co.uk
Tel: 01202 665432 Fax: 01202 666219 Int. code
(44)

USA and Canada
NBN
custserv@nbnbooks.com
Tel: 1 800 462 6420 Fax: 1 800 338 4550

Australia and New Zealand
Brumby Books
sales@brumbybooks.com.au
Tel: 61 3 9761 5535 Fax: 61 3 9761 7095

Far East (offices in Singapore, Thailand, Hong
Kong, Taiwan)
Pansing Distribution Pte Ltd
kemal@pansing.com
Tel: 65 6319 9939 Fax: 65 6462 5761

South Africa
Alternative Books
altbook@peterhyde.co.za
Tel: 021 447 5300 Fax: 021 447 1430

Text copyright Chrissie Blaze 2008

Design: Stuart Davies

ISBN: 978 1 84694 072 9

A CIP catalogue record for this book is available
from the British Library.

Printed and bound by CPI Group (UK) Ltd,
Croydon, CRO 4YY

O Books operates a distinctive and ethical publishing philosophy in
all areas of its business, from its global network of authors to
production and worldwide distribution.

No trees were cut down to print this particular book. The paper is
100% recycled, with 50% of that being post-consumer. It's processed
chlorine-free, and has no fibre from ancient or endangered forests.

This production method on this print run saved approximately
thirteen trees, 4,000 gallons of water, 600 pounds of solid waste,
990 pounds of greenhouse gases and 8 million BTU of energy. On its
publication a tree was planted in a new forest that O Books is
sponsoring at The Village www.thefourgates.com

HOW TO READ
YOUR HOROSCOPE
IN 5 EASY STEPS

Stop Reading Books (Except This One...)
and Start Reading Charts

Chrissie Blaze

BOOKS

Winchester, UK
Washington, USA

Contents

Books by Chrissie Blaze are *Workout for the Soul: Eight Steps to Inner Fitness*, AsLan Publishing, Inc., November, 2001; *The Baby's Astrologer: Your Guide to Better Parenting Is In the Stars*, Warner Books, 2003; *Das Baby-Horoskop. Die besten Erziehungstipps stehen in den Sternen* (Broschiert) Ullstein Tb; Auflage: 1 (Dez. 2004); *Power Prayer: A Program for Unlocking Your Spiritual Stength*, Adams Media, 2003 (co-author, Gary Blaze; Foreword by Marianne Williamson); and *Mercury Retrograde: Surviving Astrology's Most Precarious Times of the Year*, O Books, 2008.

I dedicate this book to my beloved mother, Phyllis Shafe. Although she passed away from this physical realm she will always be my guiding star. I love you, Mum.

PREFACE

A little learning is a dangerous thing, but a lot of ignorance is worse.

It was during the coffee break of a workshop I was conducting on *Aspects in Astrology* that I had the revelation. The room was buzzing with students talking in rapid-fire sentences and with great gusto about *squares, sextiles, septiles* and *sesquiquadrates*. I was fielding questions from five people simultaneously when, out of the corner of my eye, I saw Aimee Grant in tears. I turned to her, slightly relieved to be out of the line of fire, when she suddenly screamed: "*I can't stand any more of this. I must be stupid. I just don't understand anything!*" This silenced the room and everyone turned to stare in horror at poor Aimee. I could almost see the collective thought pattern, "*Poor Aimee, yes, indeed she must be pretty stupid.*" However, what dawned on me, as the teacher, was that I was in fact the stupid one. I had assumed everyone understood the jargon and in fact it then turned out that Aimee was not alone and half the class didn't either.

Since that fateful class I have tried to demystify astrological jargon and symbols as a key to teaching beginners' astrology. Astrology is a complex subject because it's a study of the cosmos. Like any subject – from quantum physics, to computers, to chemistry, to algebra to Mandarin Chinese or Arabic – much of the complexity is related to the jargon and the symbols. When you first look at any of these subjects, you won't have a clue what they mean until you learn the symbols.

If you persist in your study of astrology, you will soon get used to *glyphs, houses, aspects, transits* and even *sesquiquadrates* just like you understand strange words like the *Internet, websites, google* and *e-mail*. There is, however, a learning curve. I can't miraculously implant those squiggles, symbols and unpronounceable words in your brain; you will have to learn them. If you're new to astrology, it will require some effort to learn the jargon and decipher the symbols (unless you naturally have the mind and inclination of a cryptologist). The aim of this book is to present them as painlessly as possible, and so help you to understand your horoscope. After all, this is your gift from the cosmos given to you at birth, so why not use it?

After spending over twenty-five years teaching I have learned at least two things. The first is that nobody likes being talked down to. Secondly, nobody likes you to talk over their heads. In *How to Read Your Horoscope in 5 Easy Steps*, I aim to share with you on a level with which we both feel comfortable. Although this book is for the novice astrologer, I have friends who have studied astrology for years and enjoyed it. It is like playing the piano; it never hurts to keep practicing the scales. Personally, I can never resist reading yet another beginner's book, even though I've studied astrology now since I was fourteen, which I have to admit is over forty years.

One piece of good news is that constructing *horoscopes* (also known as *birth charts* or *natal charts*) is now easy compared to when I first studied astrology. This was in a byegone era – pre-computers. This was not without challenge for me, as I am neither a brilliant mathematician nor predominantly left-brain. In the good old days, we had to draw horoscopes by hand using logarithms and this level of difficulty was like a veil through which only the most motivated passed. (Having more motivation than analytical acumen, I did complete my formal training in astrology at the Faculty of Astrological Studies in London.) Now everyone has access to astrology and can construct a chart within seconds. This is one example of the simplification of the mysteries previously only available to the elite, now taking place in this Age of Aquarius.

The Astrological Ages represent changes of consciousness and each lasts about 2,150 years. The previous Age was Pisces, and Jesus was the Avatar of this Age. This great Master of Love demonstrated to humanity lessons associated with Pisces – love, sacrifice and service. According to Luke 22:10 and Mark 14:13, Jesus said: "*A man will meet you carrying an earthen pitcher of water; follow him into the house where he goes in.*"

Some astrologers interpret this to mean that Jesus was announcing the coming Age of Aetherius because the sign of Aquarius is represented by the water bearer carrying a pitcher of water. This is symbolic of the waters of truth being poured to everyone as "power to the people". The availability of astrology to everyone through computers is one aspect of this power.

There are many theories about when the Age of Aquarius actually started or when it will start. This is because the *cusp* (first piece of jargon, meaning *edge* or *beginning of a change)* of each Age lasts for over one hundred years and so it is difficult to give an exact date, although I believe it has already started and have done astrological research to this effect. When we move from one astrological Age to another, the consciousness of humanity is subjected to different influences which help to bring about a collective change. The change that is now taking place is towards a more Aquarian influence of a global humanitarian approach and the blending of science and spirituality. These are some of the positive aspects associated with this New Age.

What I dislike most about the New Age movement is an unhealthy obsession with self. In learning about your own horoscope you will at first become a bit self-obsessive but the ultimate aim is to gain a deeper understanding of yourself and others. Astrology is a tool to gain self-mastery and a reliable sense of timing. However, in these days of chaos and confusion what we do for others is the real key to our progress. Only when we give ourselves away in service to those less fortunate do we truly find who we are.

Since we are bundles of energy (solidified Sunlight) and microcosms of the universe, it follows that the cosmic energy patterns affect us. Astrology is the study of the influence of these cosmic energies on our affairs and behavior. It is an all-encompassing, liberating study that helps us develop a clear, analytical mind and a reliable intuition.

You may think it impossible to distil a cosmic science that takes a lifetime to learn into just five easy steps. However, like the White Queen in Alice in Wonderland, I like to believe in the impossible. Astrology proves that we can all achieve seemingly impossible things with a bit of faith and a lot of work.

I realize that a little knowledge can be a dangerous thing but it's also true that a little knowledge is the first step to deeper knowledge. This is the goal of *How to Read Your Horoscope in 5 Easy Steps*. It's a good introduction and overview of the astrological basics, designed so that you can start analyzing your own horoscope from Step 1. You won't learn everything you need to know about your horoscope but it will get you off the starting block to this fascinating journey of self-discovery.

Adopt an intuitive approach towards reading your horoscope and allow new concepts to rest lightly on your mind. If you don't immediately understand something don't be put off. Be open and soak up what you are reading without trying to decipher it and things will eventually fall into place. Use the creative right side of your brain as well as the analytical left-hand side. This approach is important because the ancient astrological symbols reveal truth and wisdom directly to your intuition. If you approach it in this way and learn the jargon and the symbols listed at the end of each Step, understanding will dawn.

One final word before we take this cosmic journey together. As an astrologer-to-be you have a great responsibility because others will turn to you for advice. Learning astrology is not just about analyzing horoscopes but it's also a personal journey for you to develop more wisdom, compassion, integrity and a large dose of intuition. Once you put on an astrologer's hat you will find that your words affect people so make sure they're helpful, honest and healthy. This is one reason why it's best to start by reading your own horoscope first.

You can contact me with feedback and questions via my website at www.chrissieblaze.com.

CHRISSIE BLAZE

HOW TO OBTAIN YOUR HOROSCOPE

If you don't already have a copy of your horoscope, visit my website from where you can print out a free copy of your horoscope. To find the correct page on my website, go to a search engine, such as Google, and type in http://www.chrissieblaze.com/reports.shtml. Now, scroll right down to the bottom of the page and click on "*Free chart wheel.*" This will take you to another page; scroll down again, click on the free chart wheel option and enter your birth data where prompted. In a few seconds (if the world wide web is willing) your horoscope will appear; print out a couple of copies in landscape format and you're ready to begin. If there's a problem, as there sometimes is in the Internet world, just Google "*free horoscope*" or "*free horoscope chart wheel*" and see what comes up.

ACKNOWLEDGMENTS

My husband, Gary, is so patient enduring hours of endless astrology book chat with hardly a sigh. Gary, my fellow Aries and partner in all things, you're the best. Thanks for your boundless love and support as well as your perceptive editorial advice. Thanks to Richard Lawrence, for recommending me to his publisher, John Hunt of O Books. Working with John and his innovative publishing company has been a terrific experience. Thanks to all the great astrologers who have inspired me, especially Dane Rudhyar and Steven Arroyo, and also to Kepler and Cosmic Patterns, Software, Inc. for their kind permission in allowing their horoscopes to be reprinted in this book. Finally, a special word of thanks to the late Dr George King, my amazing Spiritual Master and Founder/President of The Aetherius Society; without his incredible wisdom, genius and compassion my life would be a pale shadow of what it is today.

INTRODUCTION

"The cosmos speaks to us in mysterious ways. Astrology is a language to interpret these cosmic mysteries. The solar system is our college; the planets and constellations our teachers; the horoscope our syllabus and examination paper. When we graduate we will live more fully and travel beyond the stars."

You are unique and your horoscope proves it. There is not one other person anywhere on else on earth who has a horoscope quite like yours. Your horoscope is a gift you were given at birth and is your guidebook for life.

The word *astrology* is derived from Greek, *Astron* (Star) and *Logos* (talk). It's *Star Talk* – in other words it's a language. Astrology is the influence of the planets on human behavior and its language describes this influence. It is the language used by the cosmos to speak to us, which it does every second of every day. It is not a language of words but a visual language of symbols that communicate at a deeper level than words. This is why it's better to read your horoscope than just to read books about it. Symbols are powerful and deeply rooted in the collective unconscious. The reason why international corporations like *McDonalds* and *Mercedes Benz* use globally recognized symbols is that they evoke certain feelings and associations more directly than the words themselves.

When you look at your horoscope what you are actually seeing is a slice of the cosmos. If you could take a tuning fork to your horoscope you would find that the energy of that cosmic slice vibrates to your own personal energy pattern. Your horoscope is you, from an energy perspective.

Anna is a clairvoyant who can read your aura just by looking at you. It's uncomfortable at times because you can't keep any secrets from her, especially when she's on form! Just by looking at you, Anna can tell your mood and your health, as well as give an interpretation of your personality and what is happening in your life. In a similar way an astrologer looks at the energy pattern of your horoscope to give an interpretation. Just as a clairvoyant is employing her psychic powers so too does an astrologer, though in a different way. The clairvoyant reads your aura through the patterns and colors she sees while the astrologer reads the energy pattern of your horoscope through the planets, signs, houses and the relationships these make with one another.

Your horoscope, the chart drawn up for the moment of your birth, is a blueprint for your life and destiny. It is a guide or a road map through the highways and byways of life. It is also your karmic pattern and shows what your soul has agreed to take on before you were born.

It may seem difficult to believe that even a tiny baby is an emerging soul with lessons to learn. It's not for us to say whether this innocent child was Jane Doe or Joan of Arc but, by reading her horoscope, we can see her potential and what she could achieve in this life. After all, who you are today is more important anyway than who you might or might not have been in the past.

Astrologers don't believe we're here for just one life before we go to heaven. We believe life is a long journey through many lifetimes. Reincarnation and karma are, therefore, twin concepts used in astrology. These laws of the cosmos govern our thoughts and actions. This is not a new thought. It has been said in different ways by different people throughout the ages. Newton said in his Third Law of Physics: *"For every action, there is an equal and opposite reaction."* The Lord Buddha gave a similar teaching over two thousand years prior to Newton. In the New Testament we find the teachings of Jesus as: *"...whatsoever a man soweth, that shall he also reap."* In these modern times, the Beatles summed up karma when they said: *"The love you take is equal to the love you make."*

The karma we are constantly creating every second of every day is worked out over lifetimes. If you take an honest look back over your life now, you will probably agree it took you a long time to learn something and to change in the light of it. Sometimes we literally get knocked over the head before we realize what we are supposed to be doing with out lives. An old college friend, Michael, was about to embark on a lucrative investment career when a car accident landed him in hospital for several weeks. It gave him a chance to rethink his plans and his life. He realized his heart wasn't in his previous career choice and he later became a doctor and joined *Medicins san Frontieres* where he now works saving lives in war-torn areas.

We are gods in the making, unaware of our divinity. Our home and school is the solar system and Mother Earth our current classroom. Everything we do takes place within the beautiful mystic backdrop of the cosmos. Even our thoughts will delicately touch the remotest star in the galaxy and that remote star will also touch us.

In astrology, we are concerned with the influence of the planets in this solar system. The touch of these magnificent living entities is beneficent, urging us to evolve on our journey back to God. As we have free will, we can choose to ignore the planets' subtle, delicate energies and move out of sync with the natural flow and order of life. If we do we move away from our destiny.

Instead of blaming the planets for our misery we can use them as marvelous tools. Once we learn the mystical language of astrology as portrayed in our horoscopes, our path is revealed. We can unlock our potential, understand our karmic relationships and learn how and when to act. Astrology is a tool not a crutch. Once you develop an active, reliable, high intuition you will no longer need it. However, for most of us, it's extremely helpful.

Although you may hear otherwise, astrology is *not* fatalistic. The planets incline but they do not compel and nothing is inevitable. You can choose to overcome difficulties and limitations rather than succumbing to them. You can use astrology to help you manage your negative karma and use your positive karma more powerfully.

One great thing about astrology is that it works whether people believe it or not. Ironically, the people who scoff at astrology are the ones who are more or less ruled by it. When I first started teaching astrology a student attended my classes with his wife. I felt his main reason for coming was to scoff; he seemed to think his endless verbal jousting made him look clever. In fact it had the opposite effect. You could almost hear the silent groan that emanated from the class when he spoke, especially from his embarrassed wife. Because I was new to teaching I put up with his rude remarks which I would not do today.

I could see from this poor man's horoscope that his relationship was about to break up. Had he given astrology a chance he could have taken steps to avoid this painful split. As he didn't, he ended up losing his twenty-year marriage. I must admit I felt relieved that he no longer attended but also felt bad that I hadn't been able to convince him of the efficacy of astrology.

The more we understand astrology, the more we can avoid apparently inevitable results. Let's look at an example with the Sun and Saturn. The great life-giving luminary, the Sun, warms us. In astrology the Sun represents your vitality and is your "fuel." The mighty planet Saturn has a different effect. Astrologers of the past called Saturn *The Grim Reaper*. Today, astrologers take a more enlightened approach, referring to this wonderful planet as *The Great Teacher*. While it does bring limitation and discipline, this helps us to learn.

My strict schoolteacher taught me Latin through limiting my desire to daydream with a quick, sharp blow of her ruler to the back of my head. This would not happen in a classroom today but I can assure you it did when I was at school in England many Moons ago. I don't believe I ever would have learned Latin without it. (Not that it would have mattered too much, but that's another subject). Saturn's effect in your horoscope is rather like this, although it's more compassionate than my ruler-toting teacher! The limiting effect of Saturn may come in the form of ill health, or a restriction of some type that causes you to 'toe the line'.

When Saturn today is in that same little piece of the cosmos as the Sun was when you were born, it affects you. (These movements of the planets today over the planets in your horoscope are called *transits*). Astrologers can predict future possibilities by looking at your transits. One effect might be that Saturn, by sitting on top of your Sun energy, could deplete your vitality and cause ill health. A good astrologer would alert you to this potentially difficult period and recommend you take remedial steps such as healthy diet, exercise, positive affirmations and/or spiritual practices. If you do this you can then avoid or alleviate a patch of ill health. You are then working *with* the Saturn/Sun energies. The practical, concrete energies of Saturn incline you to *work* rather than to dream. If you work with Saturn transits, you can in turn build strong foundations in your life. If you ignore them, you will then experience the limitation of Saturn's transits head-on.

As well as helping you to be forearmed, astrology also helps you take your blinkers off. It's easy to see other people's faults but hard to see your own. It's also the same with your talents. Very few people recognize just how many skills they have at their fingertips. Self-knowledge is a blessing.

One of the ancient concepts held by the Egyptians, the Hermetic Mystery Schools and others, is that man is the microcosm of the universe – the macrocosm. In other words, we are sparks of the Divine. This also finds expression in the teaching: *"The kingdom of heaven is within you; and whosoever shall know himself shall find it."* In the words of Pythagoras, *"Man know thyself; then you shall know the Universe and God."* Conversely, if we know the Universe, it will lead us towards self-knowledge and to God. This is the true basis of astrology.

STEP 1

STOP READING BOOKS AND START READING CHARTS

While your birth data is important; a genius and a savage can share the same birth time. What is really important is your level of awareness and evolution. Astrology is a tool to help you on this journey of the soul.

What to Ask Mom

The first thing you need to calculate your horoscope is your *birth data*, the place, time and date of birth. Get this data from Mom if you can or even better from your birth certificate. Mom's memory can be a bit faulty. *"It was sometime after lunch"*; was it two minutes or two hours after lunch? A few minutes can make all the difference.

I was lucky because the first thing my Mom asked when I was born was *"what time is it?"* (They don't put the time on English birth certificates.) The nurses thought she had gone a bit loopy and kept trying to tell her she had a girl. She said: *"That's OK, that's just fine, but I need the time!"*

If you don't have your horoscope with you as you read this, you'll need to get one. I did promise that you'd stop reading books and start reading charts; I'll stick to that promise if you will.

Stop reading right now and find your horoscope. If you don't have one, don't panic. All you need is a computer. You don't even need an *ephemeris* (a table showing the daily positions of the planets) or logarithm tables. If you don't have a computer, visit a friend, neighbor, your local library or copy shop and borrow one. Don't ignore this or think you can do it later. Do it right now! Return to the Preface to find out how to download your horoscope.

Reading Your Horoscope

I trust you have your horoscope in front of you. Take a good long look at it. What's your initial impression? Does the pattern suggest anything to you? Does anything stand out? Always listen to those first impressions.

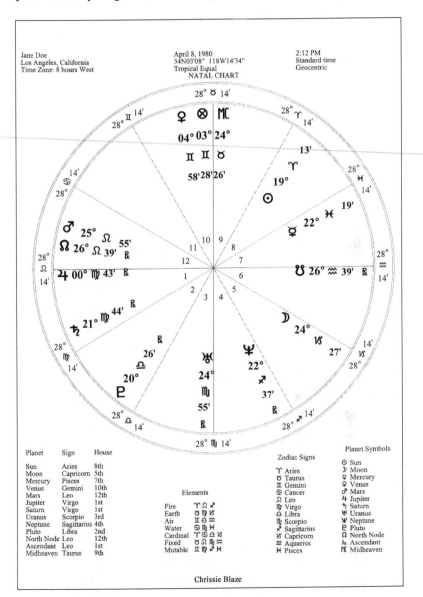

Chrissie Blaze

When I was fourteen, Aunt Esme showed me my horoscope for the first time. It was one of those weird past life moments because, without any training at all, I understood it. All the symbols and squiggles made sense to me. I have to say though, after my immediate recognition, I then had to spend years learning (or re-learning) the symbols and jargon! Perhaps you will have a similar experience. If not, don't worry. Your horoscope looks complex now but the good news is that initially you will only have to learn three main categories, the *sign of the zodiac* and *house* that each *planet* occupies, and the relationships the planets make to one another, in order to make sense of it.

The Signs, Planets and Houses in the Game of Life

Let's look at the meanings of the signs, houses and planets. Traditionally, astrologers say the twelve signs of the zodiac (signs) represent your mode of expression, the *way* you do things. The ten planets inhabit the different signs in your horoscope and they provide you with different types of energy to use; passion, determination, caution, imagination, etc. The twelve houses are the twelve segments or divisions into which your horoscope is divided. Each house is associated with a different area of your life including your finances, home, family, relationships, career and spirituality. The planets are modified again by not only the signs of the zodiac but also by the houses they occupy.

To help you understand the difference between the signs, planets and houses better, think of life as a game, or a play in which you are taking part. In the words of Sir Henry Newbolt: *"Play up, play up and play the game!"* Life isn't just something that happens to you, you can choose how to play it. The signs, planets and houses are cosmic gifts from God to help us to play the game of life. According to how we *use* them we can give a stunning performance or a lackluster one.

In the game of your life, the planets are like the actors. I'm sure you'll agree that you don't just have one note to your personality that's constant all the time. There are many different sides of you and these are like the different actors in your personal play. The leading actor or the authoritative part of you is the Sun; your inner child is the Moon; the charming, sociable part of you, Venus; the energetic, assertive part, Mars; the generous part, like a beneficent uncle, is Jupiter; the taskmaster who brings discipline and structure, Saturn; the inspired part who espouses social causes, Uranus; your compassionate, imaginative part, Neptune; and the powerful magician who seeks to control and bring change, Pluto.

The signs of the zodiac are like the personalities of all these actors or the roles they play. Perhaps your leading actor is bold, decisive and forthright with a typical Aries personality. Perhaps she is quick-thinking and clever, like the Gemini; or ambitious and goal-oriented like the Capricorn. Next is your inner child. Is he stubborn but sweet and artistic like the Taurus, or is he sparkling and a bit of a show-off like the Leo?

Then finally there are the houses, associated with different areas of your life. Think of these as scenes in your play. In one scene, the leading man is behind his desk at work; in another scene he is the adventurer traveling the world. The leading man at work would be associated with the 10th house of career, and the adventurous leading man with the 9th house of travel. Keep this analogy in mind as you study the Steps in this book.

Take another look at your horoscope. What you are seeing is an Earth-centered map of the heavens at the time of your birth. It shows the planetary positions as if viewed by you at the time and place of your birth. The line that dissects the 360-degree circle into top and bottom halves, represents the horizon when you were born. The planets are drawn as symbols inside this circle. Those planets falling above the line were above the horizon when you were born; those planets below the line were below the horizon at your birth.

How the Planets Affect You
Let's begin by looking more closely at the planets denoted by symbols known as *glyphs*.

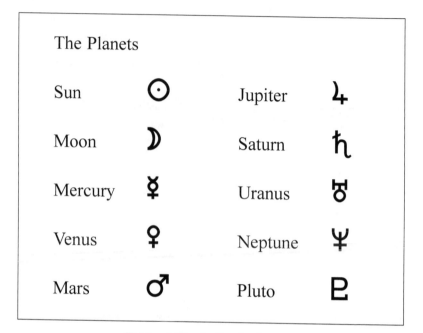

Table of Glyphs for the Planets

Astrology is a language of symbols and these translate to energy. The living planets emanate this energy for us to use in different ways. The Sun gives life, vitality and creativity, the Moon supplies us with feeling energy; these planets are known as the *luminaries*.

Mercury, Venus and Mars are the nearest planets to the Sun and the fastest moving. Mercury represents your mental energy; Venus your social energy, the energy to form relationships; and Mars your assertive energy. These are known as the *inner* or *personal planets*.

Finally, there are the *outer or transpersonal planets*. The next planet after Mars is Jupiter which provides an expansive energy to expand your pay packet as well as your waistline; after that is Saturn, a limiting, consolidating energy. Finally are the outer planets, Uranus, Neptune and Pluto. These planets move more slowly and have a generational influence. While still affecting you personally they also affect your entire generation. Uranus provides the energy for change through revelation and inspiration; Neptune, the energy of the mystic and imagination; and finally, Pluto, the energy for transformation. On the subject of Pluto, you may have heard that it was demoted from its planetary status by astronomers in 2006. Despite this it is a very powerful planet in astrology.

In your horoscope each planet is located in one of the signs of the zodiac. Planetary positions are measured by degrees, minutes and seconds. Take a look at your horoscope and at the planetary glyphs. Next to each glyphs are numbers that indicate its position in the sign it occupies. (Some chart wheels may not have the degrees and minutes listed. Don't worry too much at this stage. However, by Step 4 you will need to obtain a horoscope that does list the planetary degrees and minutes).

Each of the twelve signs of the zodiac contains 30 degrees. Each degree contains 60 minutes and each minute contains 60 seconds. Your Sun, for example, could be 10 degrees 12 minutes 8 seconds or 25 degrees 6 minutes 22 seconds. (Some horoscopes do not record seconds but only degrees and minutes.) The exact degree of the planets is important for measurement purposes, as you will see later.

Planetary Patterns

Now look at the pattern of your horoscope. You may have the planets bunched up together, opposite each other or all spread out around the wheel. If you happened to be born during the time of a planetary config-uration when the planets are close together in astronomical and astro-logical terms, the planets in your horoscope would appear close together.

Planetary configurations effect humanity as a whole. The tremen-dously focused energy of the planets can cause weather disruptions or global changes of different kinds. This planetary power can inspire us or incite us to violence, depending upon how we handle the energy. There are several major planetary configurations coming up between now and 2012.

Back in May, 2000 everyone was collecting things and it wasn't by chance that there were no less than seven planets lined up in Taurus, the sign of possessions. Taureans love "things" and can stockpile and hold onto them forever. One trend was collecting beanbag toys and people couldn't get enough of them. Not surprisingly, when the planets moved on, so did the fad. This just illustrates one basic aspect of a planetary configuration which also affects global consciousness at a deeper level.

How do these bundles of energy, the planets, affect you personally? If you have three or four planets in a particular house, say the 10th house of career, it literally means you focus your energy there and you probably spend a lot of time at work! Look now and see if you have any clusters of planets in your horoscope.

The late Dr Marc Edmund Jones gave us seven horoscope patterns as well as jargon to describe these patterns. The patterns (shown below) are described in his book *The Essentials of Astrological Analysis*, Trafford Publishing, 2006. The names are the *Splash*, the *Bowl*, the *Bucket*, the *Bundle*, the *Locomotive*, the *See-Saw* and the *Splay*. What do you think would be a good name for your horoscope? Are your planets splashed out or are they opposite each other like a see-saw?

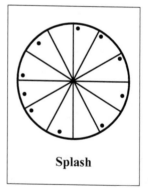

Splash

The Splash

This pattern is where the planets are scattered and spread out, occupying many signs and houses. A Splash horoscope describes an uninhibited type of personality or someone who's all over the place. Splashes tend to be a Jack-of-all-trades type, scattered and unsure about what to do. If this rings true for you, remember this pattern is only a first impression. You can find the real 'nitty-gritty' of your character delineated in the rest of your horoscope. Like all the patterns, there is a good side as well as a bad side. The Splash person has an interest in everything and an enthusiasm for knowledge. He is even-tempered, balanced and multi-talented, and can turn his hand to anything. I know a Splash person who excels at everything from the most obscure talents like picture restoration to building scientific equipment and writing poetry. Famous splash people include Ted Turner, George H.W. Bush, Carl Sagan, Nicholas Copernicus and Mozart.

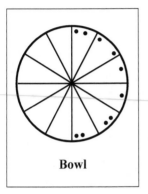

Bowl

The Bowl

This pattern describes all ten planets in one half of the horoscope. The Bowl person is different from the uninhibited Splash. She has great strength and inner power and is thoughtful, self-contained and self-sufficient. On the negative side, she may feel she's missing out on some of life's rich experiences, indicated by the houses empty of planets. She may spend time looking for this missing half of herself and trying to see the big picture. Those who have more planets on the left side are active and initiate things, while those with more planets on the right side attract things to themselves, good and bad. Typically thoughtful, self-contained Bowl type personalities are Sir Isaac Newton, Abraham Lincoln and Brad Pitt. I'm a big fan of all of these three people so Bowls can't be all that bad. In astrology you can get the worst horoscope you have ever seen, but out of that emerges the finest character. That's what makes it so fascinating.

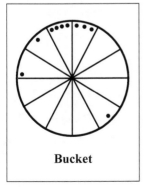

Bucket

The Bucket

The Bucket looks (well, to astrologers, anyway, who are used to seeing the sublime in the everyday and vice versa) rather like a bucket. It's actually a Bowl with a handle, with nine planets in one half of the horoscope in a group of between 120 to 180 degrees and the tenth planet opposing this whole group.

This lone opposing planet is very important in the Bucket and can literally lead the person concerned with great gusto and zeal depending on the nature and strength of the planet concerned. This is another pattern that gets a bad rap from the more "balanced" types. *"Oh, these Bucket people are extremists and zealots!"* Well, they may be but they can also be inspirational and instruments for change. Some of my favorite potential dinner party guests include John Lennon, Mother Theresa, Bill Gates, Albert Einstein and Galilei Galileo and, yes, they are all Buckets.

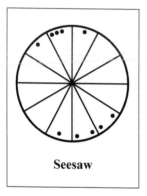

Seesaw

The See-Saw

This is similar to the Bucket but it has more than one planet opposing. Even if you see a shape that looks like a Bucket but it has two or more planets opposing the rest of the planets, it is not a Bucket but a See-Saw. You know right away from your initial glance at the See-Saw that here is a person who is in a constant state of flux, trying to find balance. It is not an easy pattern as they are always swinging backwards and forwards and bringing things up the surface. However, the See-Saw can make for another interesting personality and potential dinner party guest, brilliant, though at times exasperating. See-Saws include David Bowie, Sophia Loren, Salvador Dali and Stefi Graf; they are capable of unique achievement but may waste their talents if out of balance.

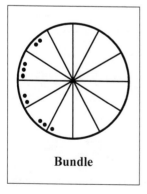

Bundle

The Bundle

The Bundle is similar to the Bowl but the planets are in a tighter group. They are usually seen clumped together into three houses in a row. Many people born in the Summer of 1955 have planets in a Bundle. This unusual group of people has some real talent with the potential to reach genius level. I'm not saying they are all budding geniuses but there's a lot of *potential* in this group. Bundles, as you might imagine, have narrow, specialized interests. This is a person who is self-contained and intensely focused, so he's not a good all-rounder. The first planet in the Bundle (the one leading from a clockwise direction) indicates the energies used to fulfill his goals. In other words, if Mars is leading he uses assertion; if Venus, charm and diplomacy. The outlook of this person is focused and an unusual ability may stem from his ability to concentrate. Budding Bundle geniuses out there should get inspired by fellow Bundles: Bill Clinton, Charles Dickens, Paul McCartney and Alexander Graham Bell.

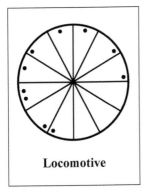

Locomotive

The Locomotive
This pattern is where one planet leads the others clockwise around the wheel and the planets are spaced at varying intervals like the cars in a train. People with this pattern have great drive and energy at their disposal. Like the Bucket, the leading planet is most significant and indicates how she might act. The leading planet also indicates a person's interest; what turns her on. The Locomotive has a low boredom threshold and indicates a compulsive personality who constantly seeks fulfillment. She has a wide variety of talents and interests but no focus unless the cluster of planets is in a single sign. If you are a Locomotive don't worry because you do have great qualities such as leadership and organizational ability. You are also in exceedingly good company. Anyone who is anyone from Leonardo da Vinci to Joan of Arc to Martin Luther King to Oprah Winfrey to the Dalai Lama is a Locomotive.

The Splay
The Splay is difficult to define. It is not like the Splash where all the

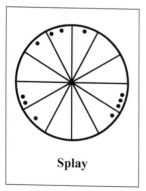

Splay

planets are spread out. This pattern is where small groups of planets inhabit very few houses. This person is an individualist who doesn't like to be regimented. He may find it difficult or even impossible to conform, being independent, driven, intense, unusual and willful. He is a unique person who follows his own path with confidence. He thrives on change and stimulation and seeks experience for the sake of it. He avoids control and restriction by others at all costs. Gosh, I could go on and on about this one because I am a willful Splay, together with some more of my favorite dinner party guests: Angelina Jolie, Hilary Clinton, Johannes Kepler, Bob Dylan and Michelangelo. What an interesting group that would make, don't you think? Certainly we wouldn't be short of a topic or two of conversation.

If you don't think your horoscope fits any of these patterns take another look. If you have some planets splayed out and others grouped together, it could be a Splash or perhaps a Locomotive. It may not fit exactly into the description but the descriptions should give you some idea. If you fall between two read them both and go from there. It's not the "be all and end all" just a helpful guide to another layer of interpretation (did I hear "*complication*"?) So you see, just by looking at the initial pattern of the horoscope you get an initial fix. Look at your horoscope now and study its pattern to gain a useful first impression.

The Signs of the Zodiac

The signs of the zodiac are the twelve basic personality types and building blocks of the zodiac. Your planetary actors express themselves according to the signs they inhabit.

Dr Edward Bach, who devised the Bach Flower Remedies, a system of energetic healing similar to homeopathy, spent years researching the different personality types by sitting on the beach in Wales. He studied how people entered the ocean. Some dived, some put one toe in, some rushed in and rushed straight out and some dithered on the edge. After years of watching people he came up with twelve major personality types. Astrology has the same basic premise.

Everyone has all twelve signs of the zodiac in their horoscope but the signs are highlighted according to which planet(s) are there. Most people know their Sun Sign, the sign of the zodiac where the Sun was when they were born, but not the signs in which all the other planets are located. Just as astrology uses glyphs for the planets it also uses symbols or glyphs for the signs of the zodiac.

Aries	♈	Libra	♎
Taurus	♉	Scorpio	♏
Gemini	♊	Sagitarius	♐
Cancer	♋	Capricorn	♑
Leo	♌	Aquarius	♒
Virgo	♍	Pisces	♓

The Symbols for the Signs of the Zodiac

If you look at your horoscope, you will see the signs of the zodiac from Aries through Pisces listed around the outside of the circle on the dividing lines or *cusp* of each of the twelve segments, known as the twelve *houses*. Below is a brief synopsis of the meaning of each of the twelve zodiac signs. I also suggest you read as much as you can about these essential building blocks by studying other books, including my book, *Superstar*

Signs: Sun Signs of Heroes, Celebrities and You by O Books, Fall 2008.

Aries – March 21 – April 19

You are spirited and assertive and others may think you're uncontrollable. You know they just don't understand you. You're meant to be ahead of the crowd, leading the way not kissing up to anyone. You don't tolerate fools gladly or anyone who tries to crush your impetuous spirit.

Taurus – April 20 – May 20

You are reliable, practical and determined with an artistic flair. Other people may think you are stubborn but it's because they lack the discernment you have. You build slowly, step by step and understand the true value of things and people.

Gemini – May 21 – June 20

You are dexterous, clever and adaptable. When people call you fickle it's because they are not as quick and intelligent as you. You like discussion, and pride yourself on being able to see every side of an argument.

Cancer – June 21 – July 22

You are nurturing, sensitive and caring. You are also moody but that's your response to the subtleties of feelings of which most are unaware. You have a psychic antenna; while others think they know, you really know.

Leo – July 23 – August 22

You are creative, noble and magnanimous. Others may think you are arrogant but their shortcomings are not your concern. You are way above the pettiness of others. You were born to lead and light up the world.

Virgo – August 23 – September 22

You are skilful, modest and discerning. While others berate you for being a critic and nitpicker, you smile knowingly at their ignorance and lack of discrimination. You are the perfectionist who understands the value of service.

Libra – September 23 – October 22

You are intelligent and courteous. You do your best to please everyone and then they criticize you for being indecisive and sitting on the fence! What an unjust world. You are the diplomat who seeks to please and bring harmony.

Scorpio – October 23 – November 21

You are deep and mysterious. People don't understand you and think you're secretive and unforgiving but you're not interested in what they think. You're already perfectly aware of your own inner demons. You are the magician seeking self-mastery.

Sagittarius – November 22 – December 21

You are perceptive and forthright. Others may think you crass as you expose their weaknesses but you know you're here to reveal the truth, whatever the cost. You are the visionary who has the intuition to see into the future.

Capricorn – December 22 – January 19

You are focused and disciplined. People think you cold as you carry out your plans for world domination. You're sure they must be lesser mortals and that eventually they will see the truth of your convictions. You have the patience and drive to accomplish anything.

Aquarius – January 20 – February 18

You are unusual and march to the beat of your own drum. If others think you weird that's their problem not yours. You are the revolutionary who can help them see the truth and to bring a better world.

Pisces – February 19 – March 20

You are kind, sensitive and imaginative. People may think you dependent and evasive but it's because they don't understand the magical place you inhabit. You are the mystic and dreamer who is at home in unseen worlds.

The Houses

Now look at your horoscope and see how it is divided into twelve segments. These segments, called houses, contain the planets and other astronomical points and are the houses. The twelve houses are drawn anticlockwise around the chart wheel. The 1st house starts on the east at the 9 o'clock position and this point is known as the *Ascendant* or *Rising Sign*. The 2nd house at the 8 o'clock position, and so on until the 12th house, the final segment. Each house is like a different room or scene in your personal play: your relationships, your career, your home, your family, and so on. Another way to think of the houses is as twelve different rooms of a mansion. There are certain places in your twelve-room mansion that you'd naturally end up spending more time in than you would the others and so it is with your horoscope.

There's a quick way to understand the *meanings* of the twelve houses. Their themes are similar to the twelve zodiac signs which are the natural rulers of the houses. The first sign, Aries, influences the activity of the 1st house, the second sign, Taurus, influences the 2nd house, and so on round your horoscope. Become familiar with the signs of the zodiac and then the themes of each house will become clearer. Like any shortcut, it is not perfect but it will get you going in the right direction.

Each house has a *natural* ruler and also an *actual ruler*. The natural ruler always rules the house and never changes. For example, the natural ruler of the 1st house is always Aries, and the natural ruler of the 4th house is always Cancer, the fourth sign of the zodiac. The *actual ruler* of your house changes according to when and where you were born, so it is specific to you.

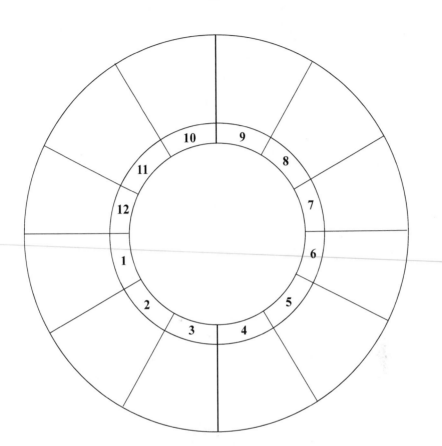

The Twelve Houses of the Horoscope

The 1ˢᵗ House - I am

This describes your personality and physical appearance and whether your hair is long and black or short and green. It's how tall you are and whether you're likely to put on weight. It's how others see you. The natural ruler of this house is Aries. This house is all about you and is the opposite House to the 7ᵗʰ, which is about your relationships. If you were born with the sign of Leo on your 1ˢᵗ house cusp (the Ascendant), you radiate the pride and confidence of Leo, with vitality and personal magnetism.

The 2nd house - I possess

The 2nd house - I possess

This house describes your sense of self worth, your value system, and explains how you earn – and spend – money. The natural ruler is Taurus. It gives an idea of what's important to you and whether you still have your cuddly toys from childhood. It is your values, as opposed to the values of another, indicated by the opposite house, the 8th. If you have Capricorn ruling your 2nd house, you are cautious and conservative with your finances but understand the value of things and how to make money.

The 3rd house - I communicate

It's how your mind works; this is your everyday, analytical mind, as opposed to your intuitive mind, indicated by the opposite house, the 9th. The natural ruler is Gemini. This is where you learn your times tables and work out your shopping lists. It is your primary education. It's also a place of movement and shows if you're light on your feet. It indicates short trips and also relationships to siblings and neighbors. If you have Aquarius ruling your 3rd house, you like to think outside the box and have a broad, objective and independent mind.

The 4th house - I feel

This is the house of home and shows if you prefer a rambling country estate or a city apartment. It is your roots and your inner self. The natural ruler is Cancer. Its opposite house is the 10th which is about you in the world, your career and vocation; the 4th is about you at home. It's also how you feel and whether you dreg up memories from the past or keep them hidden. It rules your parent, usually your mother, as well as your country and family history. If you have Taurus ruling your 4th house, you like your home to be comfortable and traditional with quality furniture and artwork.

The 5th house - I create

This is the fun house. It's your creative expression, romance and love affairs, gambling and speculation, fun and games. The natural ruler is Leo. You can see from a person's 5th house whether they are a budding Picasso and how likely they are to have children. The house also describes your children or your inner child. It's about giving love while its opposite house, the 11th, describes how you receive love. If you have Sagittarius ruling your 5th house, you enjoy sports like horse riding and archery and enjoy learning and foreign travel.

The 6th house - I analyze

This indicates the state of your physical health and your interest in this. Are you a pill-popper or do you prefer the natural way? It also describes your daily routines and interaction with co-workers if you have them. The natural ruler is Virgo. It tells of your attention to detail and striving for perfection. Its opposite house, the 12th, is about submerging the details in your quest for Oneness. If you have Cancer ruling your 6th house, your health reflects your sensitive emotions. You do well in a home-based business or like your work place to be a second home.

The 7th house - I relate

This is all about your partnerships (marriage or business). The natural ruler is Libra. It shows whether you are likely to marry and if so whether you would prefer a husband like your father or one more like your son. It's how you commit and also what you are prepared to give in a relationship. The 7th is your public relations place and your appreciation for the arts, your love of fair play and harmony. If you have Scorpio ruling your 7th house (also known as *the Descendant*), your relationships are intense, controlling and secretive. You prize emotional closeness and sharing.

The 8th house - I desire

This is your mysterious place of sex, death, sharing, rebirth, your psychic nature and transformation. If you can't see the connection it's probably because it's mysterious like its natural ruler, Scorpio. If you are married, this house indicates whether your spouse has the funds of Oprah or whether you need to support her. It's her worth as opposed to your own. On a mystic level, this house indicates your transformation as you make the ultimate surrender not to another person, but to God. If you have Libra ruling your 8th house, you want your sharing and intimate relationships to be fair and just, and on equal terms.

The 9th house - I teach

This house shows whether you are likely to be a high-school dropout or a college professor. It's the state of your higher education and also your higher, intuitive mind. You may be a high-school dropout but have the inspiration and intuition of a visionary. The natural ruler is Sagittarius. It is the opposite house to the 3rd house, your everyday mind. This house rules publishing, your philosophy of life and religious beliefs. Whereas the 3rd house is short-distance travel, the 9th house is foreign places and overseas travel. It shows your attitude to the future and to the unknown. If you have Pisces ruling your 9th house, you will dream of far away places. You are intuitive but could be an absent-minded professor.

The 10th house - I plan

The 10th house is opposite the 4th house of home and represents your public self and career. With a strong 10th house, you can be born penniless in a Third World country and end up ruling the world. The natural ruler is Capricorn and it shows your willpower, how you make your way in the world and how you are perceived in society. It indicates your ambitions and how you can reach them. It describes your father, mother or authority figure in your family. If you have Gemini ruling your 10th house, your career involves your mind and dexterity and you would make a good teacher, writer or dancer.

The 11th house - I inspire

This house is your friends and whether they are dull and reliable or extraordinary and brilliant. It shows what kind of friend you are and also your humanitarianism. It's how likely you are to join a political party and camp outside in the snow for the sake of human rights. It shows if you are motivated to join together with people of like minds in groups for the common good. The natural ruler is Aquarius. It is your idealism and vision for the future. It rules sudden events, rebellion and outrageousness. If you have Virgo ruling your 11th house, you are discriminating in your friendships and group associations, as well as loyal and helpful.

The 12th house - I heal

This last house in your horoscope is your house of self-undoing. It's not an easy place because what you are really doing is undoing all the ties that bind you to material life in your search for spirituality and enlightenment. It's also your karma, good and bad. Its natural ruler is Pisces. It is your subconscious and where you can deceive yourself. It also indicates hospitals and institutions, serving others through compassion, psychic ability and sensitivity. If you have Aries ruling your 12th house, your sense of self is connected with your spirituality. You are prepared to sacrifice yourself for God or a cause greater than you.

You have read above about the themes of each house. As mentioned, these themes of the houses are now overlaid by the signs of the zodiac on the cusp of each house of your horoscope when you were born. Look at your horoscope and see the signs dotted around the edge of the chart wheel. These signs add flavor to the activity of each house. If you have glamorous Leo on your 4th house of home you like a ritzy, expensive home with lots of dinner parties and social activity. If you have mercurial Gemini on the cusp of your 7th house, communication is important in your relationships. Stability and reliability would not necessarily be what you are seeking (depending upon other factors in your horoscope) but discussion and sharing ideas would be essential.

The House Systems

Once you have learned about the nature of the houses, and their natural and actual rulers, just to confuse you there are about thirty different methods of drawing up the houses. These are called *House Systems* and refer to a specific mathematical approach to erecting a horoscope. The good news is that no method is more "correct" than the other and astrologers have disagreed about them for years. The two most popular are *Placidus* and *Equal House* and I use both systems.

Look at your horoscope and note the name of the system which should be marked at the bottom. It is probably going to be Placidus, Equal House or perhaps *Koch*, another fairly popular system. Equal House is the easiest to understand because all the houses are equal in size. Don't worry about the house systems because the weird thing is that whichever system you use will work.

In this Step so far we have touched on the meanings of the planets, signs and houses. Just allow these concepts to rest lightly on your mind at this stage. They will be explained in more depth in later Steps.

The Elements

Each of the twelve signs of the zodiac is associated with one of the four elements – *fire, earth, air* or *water*. There are three signs of the zodiac in the fire element, namely Aries, Leo and Sagittarius; three in earth, Taurus, Virgo and Capricorn; three in air, Gemini, Libra and Aquarius; and three in water, Cancer, Scorpio and Pisces.

Fire

Aries, Leo and Sagittarius are known as the *Fire Signs*. If you have the Sun in the fire element or a predominance of fire in your horoscope, you are sparky, energetic and the life and soul of the party. You may give gentler souls a headache but you're here finding your identity and are born to initiate not follow. You are a firebrand, active, energetic and spirited. You like direct action and inspiration. If you have too much fire

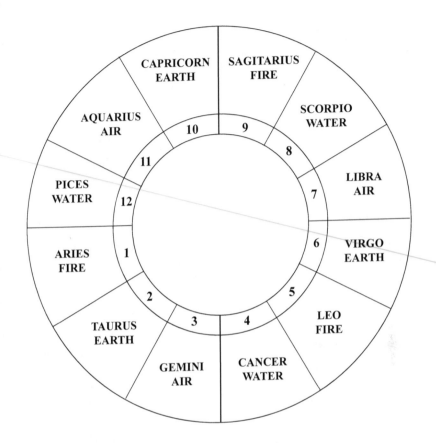

The Natural Rulers and Elements

in your chart you can be aggressive to the point of pugilism, and your enthusiasm can turn to fanaticism. If you lack fire, you lack a certain enthusiasm or *joie de vivre.*

Air

Gemini, Libra and Aquarius are the *Air Signs*. If you have the Sun in air or a predominance of this element, you are social and cerebral in your approach. While others are working on a project, you may still be discussing the right way to do it! You are intelligent and studious; born to learn and teach. If you have too much air you may be brilliant but with a tendency to be absent-minded and indecisive. If you have too little there's a lack of objectivity and perspective and, depending on other factors in your horoscope, poor communication.

Earth

Taurus, Virgo and Capricorn are the *Earth Signs*. If you have the Sun in earth or a predominance of this element, you are grounded and able to cope well with reality. While other people are wasting time chatting or generally flitting about, you are earning a living and paying the bills. You are skilful and practical with keen senses and like to smell the roses. If you have too much earth you can be a stick-in-the-mud and if you have too little or none at all you may be impractical or ungrounded in the material reality.

Water

Cancer, Scorpio and Pisces are the *Water Signs*. If you have the Sun in water or a predominance of this element, you are emotional, soulful and kind-hearted. You can be psychic and are loathe to do anything if things don't *feel* right. The more practical among us may think you are just stalling for time. Not that they understand; your world is more subtle than theirs. If you have too much water you are compassionate and kind but may live on an emotional roller coaster until you learn control of the emotions. A lack of water in your horoscope makes you rather cold and unsympathetic.

Let's look at an example of how the elements affect us. Dan was born during the time of a planetary configuration in Aquarius on 5 February 1962. This fabulous configuration inspired the Sixties song which began "*This is the dawning of the Age of Aquarius.*" On two days in February 1962 seven planets, including the Sun and Moon, were visible to the naked eye and all were lined up tightly together. In Dan's horoscope you can see all the planets bunched together in Aquarius with one planet opposing. (He had a classic Bucket pattern horoscope). This meant Dan had an over-abundance of the air element in his chart. He had a pretty difficult time as Aquarius tends to be quirky at the best of times. Dan struggled to fit in as he often shocked people with his outspoken opinions. Dan also had a streak of genius which predominantly air people sometimes have. Everyday living, characterized by the earth element, was anathema to Dan. He was the typical absent-minded professor type. You can tell a lot about a person just by the predominant element in their horoscope.

Balancing Your Elements

The good news is that you can compensate for too much or too little of any element and bring balance into your life. One simple way is to consciously attract that element into your life. I advised one 'water-less' lady client to swim on a regular basis. If you have no fire, live in sunny California or Florida or, if that's not possible, curl up by the fire. No Earth? Do physical tasks like gardening or develop a regular exercise routine. Routine is of the element of earth. If you don't have much air, take a course in public speaking to get your communication flowing. If you have too much of an element, focus on drawing the other elements into your life. This may sound simplistic but like all the best simple things, it works.

The Modalities

Finally, let's look at one more piece of jargon connected with the signs of the zodiac – the *modalities*. As you have seen, the four elements describe four distinct personality types and modify the zodiac signs. The modalities represent another modification; another layer of understanding of the signs. There are three different modalities and these are known as *cardinal, fixed* and *mutable*. Four signs of the zodiac share each modality, so there are four cardinal signs, four fixed signs and four mutable signs. Each modality is identified by special characteristics and they represent your natural way of doing things.

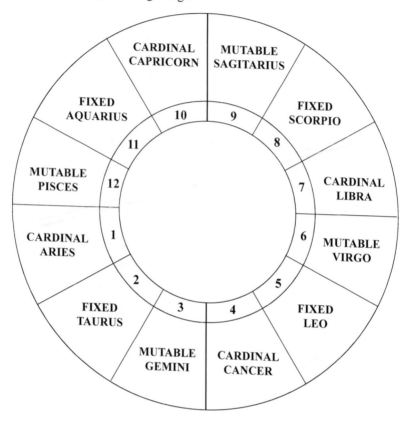

The Natural Rulers and Modalities

Cardinal

As you have just seen, Aries, Cancer, Libra and Capricorn are in different elements, namely fire, water, air and earth respectively. However, they all have something in common in that they are all *Cardinal Signs*. Characteristics of cardinal signs are leadership, independence, impatience and initiative. Cardinal people are pioneering and action-packed. People with the Sun in Capricorn, for example, initiate practical projects and make good executives. The different modalities make the elements manifest differently. For example, cardinal is an initiating energy so the assertive fire of Aries manifests rather like a jet of fire, such as a Bunsen burner.

Fixed

Taurus, Leo, Scorpio and Aquarius are the *Fixed Signs*. As you might imagine, these people are stubborn, determined, persistent and slow to change. Scorpio is fixed water, still, deep and dark like the ocean. The fixed modality has a more stable energy than the cardinal so, although dynamic Leo is a fire sign like Aries, it has a different manifestation. The fire of Leo is more like the warm glow of your fireplace in water, powerful with the feeling of security.

Mutable

Gemini, Virgo, Sagittarius and Pisces are the *Mutable Signs*. These people are flexible and resourceful but have a difficult time making decisions. They are easy going but mutable air Gemini can drive you to distraction by constantly changing his mind, while watery Pisces is more of a daydreamer. The mutable modality is changeable; therefore the fire of mutable Sagittarius is different again from fellow fire signs, Aries and Leo. While Sagittarius still has the intensity and heat of the element of fire, it is more like a flickering candle flame; changeable and adaptable blowing this way and that in the wind.

Look at your Sun and Moon signs together with their elements and modalities. You are now beginning to analyze your horoscope and are building a picture. Bear in mind that each new layer adds another dimension to your horoscope.

Step 1 Jargon

Birth data	Information needed to erect your horoscope: your place, time and date of birth
Ephemeris	Table of daily positions of the planets
Horoscope	Map of the slice of the cosmos for your

	moment of birth and place
Transits	The movements of the planets today affecting the planets in your horoscope when you were born
Natal planets	The planets in your horoscope when you were born
Glyph	Symbol
Luminaries	Sun and Moon
Personal planets	Sun, Moon, Mercury, Venus, Mars. Also known as *inner planets*.
Transpersonal planets	Jupiter, Saturn, Uranus, Neptune, Pluto. Also known as *outer planets*
Configuration	Planets aligned in the cosmos
Horoscope pattern	The shape the planets in your horoscope make These are the *Splash, Bowl, Bucket, See-saw, Bundle, Locomotive* and *Splay*
Signs of the zodiac	Twelve building block, Aries through Pisces, corresponding to twelve personality types
Ascendant	The sign of the zodiac rising in the east at your moment and place of birth. The cusp of the 1st house, also known as *Rising Sign*. Indicates your physical appearance and how you project your personality
Descendant	Opposite the Ascendant and cusp of the 7th house. Indicates how you relate to others
Houses	Twelve segments of the horoscope containing the planets and other astronomical points. They represent twelve different areas of your life
Cusp	The beginning of each house
Natural ruler	Each house is ruled and influenced by one of the twelve signs of the zodiac, its natural ruler
House system	A mathematical system of erecting a horoscope.

	There are thirty systems and the most common are called *Placidus* and *Equal House*
Elements	*Fire, earth, air* and *water*. There are three signs of the zodiac in each of the four elements
Fire Signs	Aries, Leo and Sagittarius
Earth Signs	Taurus, Virgo and Capricorn
Water Signs	Cancer, Scorpio and Pisces
Air Signs	Gemini, Libra and Aquarius.
Modality	*Cardinal, fixed* and *mutable*. There are four signs of the zodiac in each of the three modalities. The modality indicates your natural way of doing things
Cardinal Signs	Aries, Cancer, Libra and Capricorn
Fixed Signs	Taurus, Leo, Scorpio and Aquarius
Mutable Signs	Gemini, Virgo, Sagittarius and Pisces

Step 1 Exercises

- Learn the above jargon.
- Make a note of all the signs of the zodiac around the houses of your horoscope.
- Note the horoscope pattern of your horoscope.
- Note which houses contain more than one planet. Do you have empty houses?
- If a house has more than one planet, write down how that might affect you.
- Practice writing the glyphs for the planets until they become second-nature.
- Note which elements you have planets in and if you have any "missing" elements.
- Study as much as you can about the Sun signs.

STEP 2

OVERCOME YOUR BAD MOON HABITS

AND BASK IN THE SUN

There is only one thing in the world worse than being talked about, and that is not being talked about. – Oscar Wilde

When I first read the above aphorism, I thought Oscar Wilde must have had his Sun or Moon in an one of the Air signs – Gemini, Libra or Aquarius. One of the worst things for airy people is to be in a world without social intercourse, chat, talk, debate and discussion – even if it's about them. Mr Wilde did indeed have his Sun in Libra and you can see his witty, pithy weighing of both sides of the issue, so typical of this sign of the scales. A person with her Sun or Moon in Scorpio would probably never agree with Mr Wilde's aphorism. She would be likely to say the worst thing is to have nothing to feel passionate about. A Taurus Sun or Moon sign would probably say there's nothing worse than having to rush and, even worse, having no dinner.

In this Step we will look more closely at your Sun sign, Moon sign and Ascendant. These three factors alone can tell you why you are here, what you were up to in the past and what you might do in the future. We also will look at the nodes of the Moon and the angles of your horoscope.

Most astrology books begin with the Sun sign but I will begin with the Moon sign because the Moon is the first influence of our life. It most affects us when we are born and throughout our childhood.

The Moon Signs
Almost everyone knows their Sun sign but most people don't know their Moon sign; the sign of the zodiac the Moon was in when they were born. Look at your horoscope now and note the sign indicated next to the

symbol of your Moon. This is your Moon sign. Also note the degrees and minutes, as well as the element and modality of your Moon sign. Note that the Moon travels very fast and only stays in each sign of the zodiac for a few days.

Your Moon represents your past, including your infancy and past lives. It indicates the conditions you enjoyed (or endured) as a child and growing into adulthood. Your Moon sign is also your routines so it's what you keep doing over and over. It's what makes you feel safe and shows how you function in times of crisis. If you have your Moon in airy Gemini you feel secure learning and probably have several books on the go at once. Moon in fiery Sagittarius feels comfortable shooting the rapids or going out on a limb, literally as well as figuratively.

The Moon is also related to babies and when we're babies we live through our Moon signs (as does the self-centered adult who refuses to grow up). When you're a baby you don't yet know who you are. You are conscious but not self-conscious; you have personality but haven't yet developed character (represented by your Sun sign) or learned how to fit in to the world around you (your Ascendant). You do know how you feel about hunger, heat, cold, rage, fear, need. When you're hungry you scream!

Your Moon sign shows how you react; and your sense of comfort and safety – or lack of it. If you have your Moon in one of the fixed signs — Taurus, Leo or Aquarius — you will need routine to give you a sense of security. If you have a baby with a fixed Moon sign, make sure all her meals are on time! For more about this, read my book *Baby Star Signs*, O Books, Fall 2008.

It's important to know your Moon sign, because unless you are satisfying it, you won't feel happy or comfortable. If you have your Moon in the emotional, caring mutable water sign of Pisces and you work in a corporate environment in a clinical office with hard-nosed business people, you will feel out-of-sorts and uncomfortable. Your Moon will be literally out of its element, which in this case is the sensitive, feeling element of water. To feel happy, you would need to change your job or bring something else into your life that will satisfy your Moon's needs to nurture, such as charity work.

If you have the Moon in the cardinal fire sign of Aries and your life is just plain dull and boring, introduce into your routine bungee jumping, rock climbing or something daring or provocative. The fire signs are action people and they need to be on the go, mentally and physically. They like to be out in front in a leadership position of some kind because this is where they feel most comfortable.

If you have the Moon in mutable earth sign of Virgo, you need to use your skills in positive, analytical ways or you will end up complaining and feeling unhappy. You operate well behind the scenes, doing fine, detailed work. You have a natural inclination for health and healing and are extremely skilled at what you do.

If you do not find positive expression for your Moon sign, you may feel unfulfilled and then manifest the negative aspects of your Moon sign. It is much easier to be positive when you feel happy in your skin. We're now going to look at how the Moon *feels* in each of the signs and what are the needs of each Moon sign, because the Moon is all about our needs.

Moon in Aries

You need to lead and be first. Your element is fire and the modality is cardinal, so you want action, challenges and excitement. You're independent and like your own company; you would rather spend time with yourself than with someone who bores or irritates you. You are Mars-ruled with a short fuse but are excellent in a crisis, rushing in where angels fear to tread. Kiefer Sutherland, Angelina Jolie and Marlon Brando have the Moon in Aries.

Moon in Taurus

You need solid and dependable things in your life – a reliable mate, a secure job, a good meal, a nice home and a routine. Your element is earth and the modality is fixed which indicates a need for emotional and financial security. Ruled by Venus, you are pleasant, artistic and creative, and slow to anger. However, you don't like to be controlled and can lose your cool when others push your buttons. Famous Moon in Taurus people are Tina Turner, Prince Charles and Elton John.

Moon in Gemini

You need your mind to be free to roam and learn. You are the eternal student; witty and intelligent, ever alive to life and what it can teach you, and sometimes a little fickle. Your element is air and the modality is mutable. Your ruling planet is Mercury so lively discussion is essential for your good health and vitality. Actors Goldie Hawn, Gwyneth Paltrow and Jim Carrey all have Moon in lively Gemini.

Moon in Cancer

You need to be able to express your colorful emotions through story-telling, entertaining or helping people in some way. You are a born nurturer and love to cook. The Moon is at home in Cancer, giving you sensitive, strong emotions and a need for home and family. You can be irritable and a little cranky. Your element is water and the modality is mutable. Moon sign celebrities include Benny Hill, Keanu Reeves and Liza Minelli.

Moon in Leo

You need to be creative and have fun. It's a nice Moon sign for a child to have as it enjoys fun. You want to lead, to be seen as confident, noble and glamorous. You yearn for the limelight and have a weakness for adulation. Your element is fire and the modality is fixed. Your ruler is the Sun and you love to shine. A lot of celebrities share this Moon sign. Famous Leo Moons are Charlize Theron, Tom Cruise and Barbara Streisand.

Moon in Virgo

You need to be of service, but discerning in your service or others will take advantage. Your element is earth and the modality is mutable so you're practical, helpful and easy going. You are skilful and need to express your critical ability in positive ways through writing, editing or analysis, or your own highly developed critical nature may affect your health. The talented actors Robert Redford, Dustin Hoffman and Jodie Foster all have the Moon in Virgo.

Moon in Libra

You need to keep the peace. You are diplomatic, charming and sociable. Your element is air and the modality is cardinal so you're good at debate and can see both sides of an issue. Making decisions is, therefore, not your strong point. You understand compromise and do well in partnerships. Celebrity Moon in Libras are Leonardo di Caprio, Angela Lansbury and Sting.

Moon in Scorpio

You need an outlet for your intensely emotional nature. Your element is water and the modality is fixed, so your desire nature is strong. You are intense and magnetic, if not controlling, and attract people like moths to a flame. It's not surprising that some of the most charismatic actors have Moon in Scorpio. These include Elizabeth Taylor, Sharon Stone and Warren Beatty.

Moon in Sagittarius

You need freedom and adventure and you are enthusiastic and optimistic about life. Your element is fire and the modality is mutable which makes you restless, always wanting to travel and be on the move. You are forthright and a little "preachy'", with a need to make your opinions heard. You yearn to know the deeper answers to life. Celebrity Sagittarius Moons are Nicole Kidman, Jennifer Aniston and Albert Einstein.

Moon in Capricorn

You need responsibility because you are ambitious and yearn for success. You can be hard on yourself and others with your intense focus and discipline, but can achieve anything you set your mind to. Your element is earth and the modality is cardinal. You are cool as a cucumber and handle crisis well. You have integrity and are thoughtful. Great actors with the Moon in Capricorn include Brad Pitt, Kim Basinger and Johnny Depp.

Moon in Aquarius

You are quirky and original and need to surround yourself with friends. You need to be unpredictable and original in your approach. You are interested in people but in rather a detached way like an entymologist studying an insect. Your element is air and the modality is fixed so you are sure of your opinions. Famous people with Moon in Aquarius are John Lennon, Uma Thurman are Britney Spears.

Moon in Pisces

You need an opportunity to express your compassion, sensitivity and imaginative approach to life through music, charity or the arts. Your element is water and the modality is mutable so you can be evasive, sentimental and mystical. You are easily moved and like to help those less fortunate. Famous people with the Moon in Pisces include Ricky Martin, Michael Vartan and Cindy Crawford.

While your Moon sign represents your needs and what makes you feel comfortable, it is also your past. Although you must satisfy your Moon needs to be happy, you are here to embrace your Sun sign.

The Sun Signs

Your Sun sign is important because it provides you with the vitality and creativity you need to evolve and to develop character. I have heard people say, as if to disprove astrology, *"Well, I have read some astrology books but I'm nothing like my Sun sign.*" My answer to them is: "*You should be.*" People who're nothing like their Sun signs are not living up to their potential.

The reason we are here is not just to work and pay bills but to learn and evolve through love and service. We choose a particular Sun sign so we can use the qualities and learn the lessons that sign offers to us. It is a cosmic gift we accept before we're born. We owe the Sun a lot because without it, we wouldn't be alive. The more we understand and consciously use the energy of our Sun sign the stronger and more magnetic we become.

A good way for you to center yourself from an astrological perspective is to consciously draw on the power of your Sun sign. As we grow and mature, we move away from our more childlike responses towards a place of integrity and character represented by our Sun sign.

I have a strong, stubborn Moon in Taurus and when I was a child if I didn't like someone, I would poke out my tongue at them. A typical child-like reaction or, astrologically-speaking, a typical Moon sign reactive response! As I grew older I found that response was just not appropriate (though I have to say I sometimes feel like doing it.) In some ways, as we mature, we move towards what may seem like a less honest place. We still may not like the person our poked tongue was aimed at but now we don't show it. Society compels us to cover up our dislike and while it's great to be civilized, this can result in under-the-surface anxieties and even complexes. However, it's not really a place of less honesty; as we grow and mature we choose to *act* with integrity and compassion rather than to *react* emotionally. Now we realize that, by poking out our tongue, we are the ones who are the fools.

Your Sun sign is akin to that mature part of you that wants you to take the high road and to act instead of reacting. It doesn't want you to stuff your dislike of another person under the carpet, but it urges you to say boldly to that person "*I don't like what you just did.*" According to your Sun sign you will do or say that in one of many different ways. The higher path of your Sun sign is not an easy path to take but it's a more powerful and fulfilling one.

The Sun is the core of your being; it's your self-expression and your sense of self-worth. On the negative side, it's where you self-sabotage; it's your self-centeredness and all words that begin with "self". It's what you're learning to develop. Your Sun sign gives a strong sense of who you are and your capabilities. It is your identity.

So when people say: *"I'm nothing like my Sun sign,"* I know right away they have a lot of work to do in finding themselves.

Sun in Aries

If you have the Sun in Aries you're crackling with energy and excitement. You're an action junkie who thrives on change. You don't mind being controversial because to you the worst nightmare is to be bored. Like Aquarians you have a tendency to stir things up when life goes a bit flat and enjoy a good debate or fight. Unlike Libra who likes to please, Sun in Aries usually couldn't care less about what other people think. While this is a good quality, you can go too far, thumbing your nose to anyone who opposes what you do. You are here to lead, to inspire, to fight for justice and truth, to be your own person, honest, sincere and true.

Sun in Taurus

Sun in Taurus people are solid and dependable with an artistic side to your nature. Unlike some of the more fickle signs, you can stay with a mate, a job or a routine forever. Say no more; there is a great need for emotional and financial security. My Aunt Meredith has the Sun in Taurus and even though the rest of her horoscope is pretty sparky with lots of action-packed fire signs, she spent most of her life waiting patiently by the side of her controlling husband until the poor man passed away. Then you should have seen Aunt Meredith! At the age of 74, she embraced her artistic nature and learned to paint. With her adventurous Moon in Sagittarius she then traveled the world painting landscapes in many beautiful countries from Italy to New Zealand. She was loyal and true for over thirty years but now that Fred was gone she was free to express who she really was. You are here to build foundations for a better, more beautiful world.

Sun in Gemini

You often see Sun in Geminis at the local bookstore/coffee shop with a book in one hand and a double expresso in the other. These aren't home bodies; they like to be out and about. If you have this Sun sign, you are intelligent and talkative. You are the eternal student; ever alive to life and what it can teach you. You feel stuck if there's no growth in your life. The problem with this Sun sign is that there is never enough time for you to learn all there is to learn. There are also never enough bookcases to hold all the books you are reading. You need to express your constant thoughts and ideas and a moody, silent partner is not for you. You are lively, adaptable and feel at home in the car and on the move. You are here to learn, to communicate and to teach.

Sun in Cancer

If you have the Sun in Cancer, you are here learning about the world of feelings. Sensitive and intuitive, you follow your gut as well as your head. You feel comfortable with comfort; big recliner armchairs, soft carpets and warm, mellow people. You express your emotions through story-telling or helping people in some way. Your home is your security and you feel secure by creating a home wherever you go. Like the crab, you literally carry your home around with you. My ex-boss, Charles, had so many photographs of his family in his office that there was no room left on his desk for work. It was very clear what his priorities were. However, don't be fooled by the home-loving Cancer. They may be the provider of doughnuts and cookies, as Charles was, but they also know how to handle and hold on to power. They are here to protect and nurture.

Sun in Leo

I have a friend with the Sun in Leo who went through a really dark patch in her life on all levels – health, emotions and finances. Daniella struggled through this gloomy period for several years but only her closest friends realized it. She always looked immaculate with her Armani suits and stylish haircuts. Leos are great actors and although expressive by nature, they feel far more comfortable putting on a good show than spilling the beans. Leos like to look good and bask in the Sun and in the limelight. They are dynamic characters who like to be seen as confident, noble and magnanimous. They are masters of the grand gesture and can be arrogant but never petty or underhand. They are here to lead and inspire not to follow the crowd.

Sun in Virgo

With the Sun in Virgo you can be as efficient as clockwork but easily stressed out with your delicate nervous system. A Virgo client had three demanding, obnoxious kids and two demanding husbands (one ex, I hasten to add). She would arise at the crack of dawn, organize breakfast and lunch for everyone, get the kids and husband off to school and work and then go to her own demanding job. In between times, she wrote a book and had another child. She helped out regularly at a local soup kitchen until one day she collapsed in a nervous heap. She never could work out why. If you are a Virgo do take regular breaks, avoid letting others take advantage of your good nature and build up your self confidence. You're just about near perfect, intelligent, discerning and practical. You need to express your critical ability in positive ways or you will become the constant critic of yourself and others. You are here to be of service but be discerning in your service or others will take advantage.

Sun in Libra

As a Sun in Libra you are diplomatic, charming and sociable and, unlike your opposite, the Aries Sun, you really do care what others think. You are prepared to submerge your own viewpoint and opinions for the good of the whole. You are prepared to compromise for the sake of the relationship. You can be strong and feisty, especially in verbal debates. You do, however, have an annoying habit of standing on the sidelines not knowing which side to choose. Decision-making is not your strong point. There is, however, one thing that really upsets you and brings out your fighting spirit and that is when your ingrained sense of justice is offended. Then you will fight – and win! The Libran is *"the iron fist in the velvet glove."* You are here to bring justice and harmony.

Sun in Scorpio

Like your opposite number, Taurus, you too are fixed, stubborn and loyal. However, unlike earth Taurus, you are fixed in the water element and this brings a mysterious kind of character deep like a Scottish loch. Nobody can ever completely know all the depth and complexity of your emotional nature. It's doubtful whether you really understand it yourself. You react with self-contained, coiled power. Others may be wary of you but they don't know why. It's probably because they instinctively feel you're dangerous. If you cross a Scorpio they will never forget it. Like all the fixed signs, your magnetism is tangible and in your case, sexual. You like to feel powerful and in control. You need an outlet for your intensely emotional nature or it will turn against you and plague you with feelings of guilt, jealousy and fear. However, you have the power to heal and are here to transform yourself and others.

Sun in Sagittarius

If you want a fun person to have around, choose the Sun in Sagittarius. You're warm and your glow is like the candle. You're vital and full of life. You need freedom and adventure as you are restless, enthusiastic and optimistic. However, like all the *dual signs* (these are Pisces, Gemini and Sagittarius, each ruled by two planets) there are two distinct types of Sagittarian. The second type is studious and may be a bookworm.

Remember, Sagittarius is the natural ruler of the 9th house and that is your higher mind, philosophy and religion. If you have Sun in Sagittarius you probably have a bit of all this in your character: studious as well as athletic; a bookworm and a religious zealot. Remember, the mutable signs are hard to pin down. You are here to ask the deeper questions – and seek the answers.

Sun in Capricorn

If you are Sun in Capricorn you are not focused on having fun and frivolous things but on achieving your ambitions. This is what really turns you on. You can leave the fun until you become that hotshot lawyer or company president or whatever you want to be. You're cautious and practical and you're good at initiating projects. This means you know how to make money and gain success. Even as a child you were mature and sought responsibility while your playmates built sandcastles. While they were giggling in the sunshine, you were learning to take charge (unless your Moon sign indicated otherwise). Status and success are deep needs for you but underneath there's a lack of confidence. At some point you will learn that true confidence comes when you learn integrity, honor and truth. You are here to become a knight (or dame) in shining armor.

Sun in Aquarius

I know several people with the Sun in Aquarius and they like to work in teams or with friends. Unlike, their opposite number, Leo, they don't seek the limelight for themselves but seek to join their efforts with others of like minds. However, like Leo, Aquarius also has leadership ability and functions well as Captain of the team if he can learn to listen to other people's points of view and stop being so opinionated, thinking he's always right. If you're Aquarius, listening is not your strong point. You think outside the box and can be inventive and original in your approach. You have an affinity for astrology, quantum physics, radionics or any of the "new" sciences. You can be erratic and quick tempered with an occasional flash of intuition or even genius. You are objective rather than subjective, rational and bright, with a need to be honest and straight-forward. You don't want a purely personal life and are here to bring social justice and a brotherhood of man.

Sun in Pisces

If you're a Sun in Pisces, you're kind and compassionate and easily moved to tears. Your element is water and you like small pets and stuffed animals and all things cuddly. You need an opportunity to express your compassion, sensitivity and imaginative approach to life through music, charity or the arts. If you don't you could end up an emotional mess and take to alcohol or drugs; anything to dull the pain of your overly-sensitive nature. Unlike your opposite sign, Virgo, who knows how to create boundaries, you do not. You are like a psychic sponge, mopping up everyone's mess and feeling their pain. Don't worry, it's not all bad, in fact it's very good. You're a natural mystic and healer and are here to unlock your psychic and spiritual nature.

Combining Your Sun and Moon Signs

You now know a little about your Moon sign and Sun sign and the difference between them. The next step is to combine the two because understanding your horoscope is all about blending the different compo-nents together. It's rather like baking a cake; first you gather the ingre-dients and then you blend them together until finally you can taste the delicious cake. Are you a frosted coffee cake with caramel filling or a boiled fruit cake? Since there are 144 ingredients by combining just the Sun and Moon signs (twelve Sun signs and twelve Moon signs) we can't go through them all but I will analyze a few. Once you really learn the different Sun and Moon signs, you will then be able to combine them yourself.

First look at the elements of your Sun and Moon sign. When they are in harmonious elements, such as earth and water or fire and air, for example with a Capricorn Sun and Pisces Moon, there is ease. This means that what your Sun sign needs for self-confidence, the Moon provides. What the Moon needs for security, the Sun creates. There's harmony between your male and female sides and an understanding of the opposite sex, together with a good relationship between your mother and father.

When your Sun and Moon signs are in disharmonious elements (fire and water, water and air or earth and air) there's some interesting and also some disturbing stuff going on as you struggle between what you need (Moon) and how you want to be (Sun). A fiercely independent Aquarius Moon with a dependent Pisces Sun might say of a close, emotional relationship: "*I shouldn't need that. I'm way too strong and independent to have that needy woman in my life.*" I have a forthright Aries Sun pushing me to be first and to go where angels fear to tread together with a reserved Taurus Moon. My Moon acts like a brake, stopping me from being too impulsive. From this you can see how disharmony can be a good thing in that it can slow you down and keep you from danger. If I had ignored my Moon's need for security in favor of my danger-loving Aries Sun, I would be traveling the world as a starving author, relying on the stars to earn a crust.

What if you are an adventurous Sagittarius Sun with reticent Moon in Cancer? I have a friend, Emma, with this combination and she is an athletic go-getter but is humiliated by the perceived weakness and insecurity of her Cancer Moon. I say "perceived" because a Cancer Moon is not weak; it is just not strong in the way the fire signs are. It is extremely strong in the area of feelings, psychic sense and emotions. The thing to remember with water is that it covers the earth, puts out fire and saturates the air. It is certainly not weak but is often misunderstood because water signs are attuned to that part of life that is not visible. As with Emma, it is where we feel vulnerable.

Instead of Emma feeling good about her conflicting Sun and Moon she tells me it's like having two separate parts of her personality that disagree with each other. I'm sure we all know that feeling ...! Ms Emma

Cancer Moon goes on a trip and insists on taking the same tea Mum serves at home. She also has to have fruit cake with the tea (because she happens to be English and we like fruit cake with everything). Ms Cancer Moon is frequently appalled by her Saggie Sun's overly rash actions. She bemoans how she quit a very secure but boring job just when the pension plan was building up. Her Sagittarian Sun couldn't stand the job even more even though her Cancer Moon was desperate for that security.

Take a look at your own Sun and Moon sign and read about each of their characteristics, their elements and modalities and see if you think they blend together – or not. Even if it looks like an unholy alliance, consciously give room for both to have expression in your life.

The Ascendants

The third piece of this jigsaw puzzle is your Ascendant or rising sign. Remember, this is the 9 o'clock position on the eastern side of your horoscope and the cusp of the 1st house. The Ascendant changes signs about every two hours hence the importance of an accurate birth time. At 1:00 p.m. you could have Cancer rising, by 2:10 p.m., it could be the next sign, Leo. Check to see which sign of the zodiac is on your Ascendant.

You have already seen that the Sun in Aries has similar qualities to the Moon in Aries but the person born with the Sun in this sign is here to develop the positive characteristics of this warrior sign whereas the Moon person has already done so. The Moon is your emotions, routines and what you need to be safe; your Sun sign is your character and what you are here to develop. Your Ascendant is the filter through which you interact with your environment, it represents your physical body and so indicates health tendencies; it's the first impression you make on others.

It is like a mask or shield that you put on so that you can interact safely with your environment and the people around you. Think of it as a role you play. It is how you are typecast by your family as a child. You may be the popular, glittering Leo Ascendant who aunts adore or the pretty Libra rising who always says the right thing.

Your Ascendant is how you present yourself to the outside world. It is actually like a filter through which the energies of the planets are focused on the material plane. It is like a protective covering you wear; the uniform you take off in private. Without your Ascendant to protect your self esteem, you feel naked.

Aries Ascendant
Early in life you were typecast as the independent child and you are inclined to stick to that role as you grow into an adult. Others see you as an action-packed doer rather than a planner. You are forthright, impulsive and direct and like to act decisively and with little fuss. You are quick to lose your temper and quick to regain it. You are enterprising with a youthful charm. Your Ascendant rules the physical body, and your health tendencies are towards headaches and sinus or eye problems or rashes on the face. You have broad shoulders, slim hips and a distinctive, quick way of walking. What is good for your health is the ability to be self-motivated and independent.

Taurus Ascendant
You have a practical, steady approach to life and a resistance to change. Others see you as slow, careful and rather fixed in your ways. You are very aware of your physical environment and attuned through your senses to how things look, smell and feel. Security is important to you, especially as far as relationships are concerned. You are loyal to those close to you, regarding them like precious possessions. Unlike Aries Ascendant, you value peace and the tried and true. You are physically strong and may gain weight through water imbalance. You have a strong voice and a tendency to health issues of the throat and neck. What is good for your health are steady, safe routines and opportunities to express your artistic nature.

Gemini Ascendant

You are the family clown with your witty, fun-filled ways, and this is the mask you wear. You see the world around you as a school, filled with things to learn. You are curious and like to roam about freely asking questions and mingling with other people in social ways. You exude an air of impatience; you're quick off the mark and have a way with words. You are interesting and chatty, cool and clever, relying on your mental agility to get you through life. You have good powers of observation but a short attention span. You are light and agile in build and your health issues may be connected to the shoulders, arms, the breath and nervous system. What is good for your health is the freedom to express yourself.

Cancer Ascendant

You are a home-body who seeks security and safety in your surroundings. You appear to others as gentle and familiar. You don't walk into a room boldly but rather weave in as if attuned psychically to your environment, which you are. You like places you know and if you are in a new place, your first instinct is to protect yourself by being withdrawn or shy. You are caring and sweet and appear unassuming but can be hard to really get to know. You seek strong, successful relationships. Physically, you are inclined to be soft with a tendency to weight gain, especially as you love food! Your health issues may be digestive, intestinal ones. What is good for your health is emotional support of true friends and loved ones.

Leo Ascendant

Even as a child you were self-conscious but also confident and acutely aware of others. You feel that life is a stage on which you have to act the leading role. You have drive, staying power with a tendency to excess. You are also noble, generous, warm and enthusiastic and this helps others overlook your rather bossy character. You need to be admired for your strength and leadership and like to make things happen. You have a strong physical constitution and pride yourself on being youthful and attractive.

Leo rising people usually have a strong, healthy mane of hair, like the lion. Health issues of Leo include the heart, liver and spleen, as well as possible eye problems. Overall, you have a strong vital constitution. What is good for your health is to love and be loved, and to have plenty of fun-filled opportunities to shine and be creative.

Virgo Ascendant

Virgo rising people have an intelligent, efficient and reserved manner. If you have this Ascendant, you have a modest, quiet charm with a lot to offer once people get to know you. You are analytical and acutely aware of your environment and like to analyze situations and people before committing yourself to action. You do, therefore, come across as cool at first impression. However, you can be the most helpful and kind people of all underneath that reserved air. You have a tendency to worry and notice things that others overlook. You are health conscious and make an effort to be fit and healthy and can be quite picky with food. If you can keep your mind clear and healthy, you can keep you body the same way. Your health tendencies are connected to the abdomen and intestines, as well as colds, flus and allergies. Safe routines, gentle exercise and massage are particularly good for your health.

Libra Ascendant

This is a popular Ascendant; everybody loves a Libra rising person. You come across as pleasant and fair, attracting other people to you effort-lessly. You can be persuasive at the soft sell and quite strong once you make up your mind. However, making up your mind is not the easiest thing for you to do. Despite your charm, you may have problems in relationships as you are attracted to more competitive personalities who can see through your sweet side to the real you. Like the rest of us, you have a few flaws; though like to keep them hidden from public view. You are good looking with pleasant, even features and a winning smile. Libra rules the kidneys and the skin. Health issues can be lower back and problems caused by too much sugar or sweet food. What is good for your health are balanced relationships that bring harmony and peace.

Scorpio Ascendant

If you have Scorpio Ascendant you come across as a magnetic person with a lot of presence. You have strength which commands respect. You are usually quiet but have an inner power and determination that shines through. You have a psychic antenna that seems to see through people and their problems, to the heart of the matter. If you have this Ascendant, you do not like superficiality and are drawn to down-to-earth, natural types. You like to control your environment and the people in your orbit and are a good strategist. You are patient and reliable. You have a strong constitution and can heal yourself as well as others. Health issues may be in the area of the reproductive organs and you may suffer from headaches, infections and fevers. What is good for your health is a safe outlet for your emotionally intense nature.

Sagittarius Ascendant

With this Ascendant, your world is filled with adventure and optimism. You are willing to explore and experiment and always seem to be seeking something just over the rainbow. You are direct but also likeable, so people forgive your bluntness. You are wise and have a lot to offer. Growing up you were the one who kept everyone laughing with you antics and you are still a big child. You find humor in life which is a wonderful thing for all around you. Ruled by Jupiter, you are larger than life and your physical body may also be large due to excessive consumption of rich food and drink. Your health issues tend to be in the region of the sciatic nerve and you may suffer from diseases of the hip and thighs. Exercise is particularly good for you as you have a deep need to be active.

Capricorn Ascendant

Capricorn rising people initially appear serious but they sometimes have a hilariously funny side. In fact quite a few comedians have this Ascendant. You have a competent manner and, like Leo Ascendant people, don't find it hard to impress other people and get that job! You also look good with a quiet, conservative style that oozes success with your designer suits and Italian shoes. You project success and success comes right back to you. However, it doesn't come easily; you work hard for it. You are the responsible one in your family. Even as a child you were mature and took control of situations. Underneath your cool exterior may be an inner struggle that you are not doing enough, and anxiety about the future. Capricorn rules the joints and knees, teeth and bones. Your health issues may be back or teeth problems. Massage is particularly beneficial to you to help you relieve stress.

Aquarius Ascendant

If you have Aquarius Ascendant, you come across to others as unique and original. You are definitely an individual who's hip, savvy and intelligent. You dress in a way that is uniquely you, starting trends and fashions rather than following them. You don't want to fit in; you prefer to be seen as the individual you are. You are an idealist with an interest in astrology, metaphysics and the new sciences, and anything that is connected to the advancement of the human race. You are usually good at puzzles and at fixing things. You may be quiet but you are definitely provocative with a stubborn streak. You are friendly and seek freedom in your relationships. Health issues of this Ascendant may be connected to the circulation and nerves. You are also rather accident prone. It is beneficial for you to seek peaceful surroundings that allow you freedom.

Pisces Ascendant

This rising sign can blend into to any situation or environment, chameleon-like. You come across to others as a mystic who is changeable and kind with dreamy eyes. It's hard to pin a label on you because you are restless and one day may be open and chatty; the next quiet and introvert.

You are attuned to the subtle levels of life that others do not see or feel. You approach life with a psychic antenna which allows you to sense danger and feel people's reactions. You are hugely impressionable and subjective, feeling your way through life. You are charming and soft; you cannot tolerate too much harsh discipline or structure as it is limiting to your mystic soul. Health issues may be connected to the feet, as well as allergies and sensitivity to drugs. Stable, practical relationships are important to good health, as well as gentle exercise like swimming or yoga.

Combining Your Moon and Ascendant

Your Ascendant and Moon are complementary parts that collude to protect you from showing too much vulnerability. Together, they strengthen your armor which is a vital survival factor in this harsh world.

However, there can be a downside if your Moon and Ascendant are incompatible. If you are a person who covers up your sensitive Moon feelings and needs, you risk illness. Your Ascendant can then aid and abet you in this emotional avoidance and make things worse. An example is a tough Aries Ascendant and work-until-you-drop Virgo Moon. Both these signs are driven and neither will offer you much slack.

Another disharmonious example would be the Libra Moon who wants everything with the approval and participation of others together with the Capricorn Ascendant who was raised to tough it out alone. With awareness, even the most disharmonious elements of your horoscope can give you strength and power.

If you have a harmonious Moon and Ascendant such as a Cancer Moon and Pisces rising you have a better chance of getting your needs met. The gentle Pisces Ascendant assumes a sweet, rather helpless pose that entices others to nurture and look after them, which is just what Cancer Moon wants. Like anything good this can also be a greased slide. It can produce an extremely compassionate person or an addictive person-ality.

Take a look at your own Ascendant and Moon sign and read about each of their characteristics, their elements and modalities and see if you think they blend together – or not. Even if it looks like an unholy alliance, consciously give room for both to have expression in your life.

Combining Your Sun, Moon and Ascendant

The Sun, Moon or Ascendant in the same sign each behave similarly but with different motivations. A Capricorn Sun, Moon and Ascendant may each overwork but for different reasons. If you have a Capricorn Sun, your self esteem is tied in with your ambition and sense of duty. If you have a Capricorn Moon, a job well done makes you feel secure. A Capricorn Ascendant, on the other hand, overworks because you want to be seen as mature, competent and responsible.

Picture your Sun, Moon and Ascendant as a trio of actors in your personal play. Perhaps your Moon and Ascendant work well together, and the Sun may be the odd one out. If your Sun and Ascendant are both harmonious, your Moon's security needs may take a back seat.

Let's look at a scenario so you have a better idea of how these three characters work together. Imagine you go for a job interview. You are overqualified but need the job. You're a teenager with the Sun in Aquarius, Moon in Cancer and Leo Rising. Your elitist and rebellious Aquarian Sun nature is disdainful of having to work under someone else and the job in question is far too humdrum for your liking. What you really want is to be a rock star but Mom insists you take the ring out of your nose and color your hair back from its current dyed purple to its natural brown and put your best foot forward.

Having the Moon in Cancer you're a bit of a Mom's boy anyway, so you reluctantly agree. You really don't want to cause her any problems and need to pay her some rent money anyway. Fortunately for you, Leo Ascendant can put on a great show when it needs to and your boss-to-be is mightily impressed with your sparkling personality, self confidence and take-control attitude. Your Ascendant allows you to put your best foot forward and amazingly you act out the role of a responsible employee almost perfectly.

The interviewer is so impressed that he offers you the job on the spot. A week later, however, your new boss is shocked when you show up late for work with your ring nose and purple hair back. Even though Leo rising helped you get the job, and even though the job was necessary for your sensitive Cancer Moon, it wasn't what your unpredictable, quirky Sun sign wanted. It sounds complicated but then life is. We're here learning to satisfy all those different parts of our nature. Astrology helps us to do that without disrupting the apple cart.

Take a look at your Sun, Moon and Ascendant, and read about each of their characteristics, their elements and modalities. See how you think they blend together – or not. Remember, you can consciously give room for each of these to have positive expression in your life.

The Nodes of the Moon

Now let's look at the *Moon's nodes*; my favorite little points in astrology. These astronomical points, the *north node* and the *south node*, also known as the *dragon's head* and *tail*, are not planets but sensitive points on the *ecliptic*. The ecliptic is the apparent path of the Sun and planets through the heavens as seen from the Earth. The two nodes mark the points where the Moon's orbit around the Earth crosses the ecliptic.

The North Node /The South Node

The significance of the nodes was underestimated in old astrology but this has now changed. Many astrologers now rank the nodes on the same level of importance as the Sun, Moon and planets. This is because the nodes are destiny points. The north node represents what you are here to achieve while the south node represents what you bring from your past lives. The two nodes are exactly opposite each other in your horoscope. If your north node is 6 degrees 24 minutes Scorpio, your south node is therefore 6 degrees 24 minutes Taurus (the sign opposite to Scorpio).

The north node is like the lodestar that points the way towards your soul growth and evolution. The sign that holds the north node reveals the *flavor* of your karma in this lifetime; its house placement shows the area of life you need to develop or in which you need to become more aware. Past life connections and hangovers are represented by your south node.

Because the nodes are always in opposite signs, they are rather like a see-saw. If you have Aries/Libra nodes you desperately want relationships (Libra) and then end up feeling stifled when you get them, as you also need the freedom to be yourself (Aries). The south node, suggests overdeveloped character traits that are easy to fall back on, but they undermine you if you hold on too tightly. It's also a place of desire. You want what is represented by your south node because it's familiar. The north node suggests the qualities you need to develop, so they are unfamiliar.

The nodes are also life lessons. If you work on these lessons you will be fulfilled. If you don't, you will feel miserable and stuck. Even if you don't work on the lessons of your nodes, events will force you do so. People usually begin to work on north node lessons in their thirties whether they are aware of them or not.

If you consciously work on the lessons of your north node, life will push you more quickly towards your destiny. It is like taking the more difficult higher road, rather than the more familiar lower road. It's not an easy path and you may feel awkward and uncertain because the path is new and untested. It is, however, the one your soul is urging you to take. Look at your horoscope and note the sign and house position of your own north and south nodes.

The Nodes through the Signs of the Zodiac
North Node in Aries/South Node in Libra
Co-dependency and a tendency to have problems in relationships are issues for you. One of your lessons is to love yourself and to trust your

instincts. You have spent past lives sublimating your independence in order to keep the peace for the sake of other people. Now you are here to find who you are, to express yourself and to act decisively and independently in a leadership role.

You may have an innate fear of expressing your independent wishes and asserting yourself because you prefer the comfort of being considered "good." However, strive to be brave and confident in yourself rather than the person other people would like you to be. Learning to act confidently on your impulses is one of the lessons of this position.

One of your fears is that you might end up alone. Only when you truly learn independence, will you have balanced and loving relationships. Instead of striving for peace and harmony in relationships, strive for inner peace. This will improve your relationships and bring you fulfillment.

Your destiny is about bringing out the best of the sign of Aries: leadership, independence and being your own person. Whenever you have decisions to make, be brave and make your decision in the light of your north node. Act from what you feel is right, not what others feel you should do. Rely on yourself rather than relying on what others tell you.

This description also applies if you have your North Node in the 1st house.

North Node in Taurus/South Node in Scorpio

You have great intensity and the desire for extreme emotional situations which draw you into exciting and sometimes dangerous close associations. You have a tendency to define your own worth and values through the power of a significant other. If you are not married or in a close relationship, you may still be wrapped up in the needs of others at the expense of your own needs. Because of this, you attract intense life situations which wrap you up emotionally and drain your inner peace. You cannot develop self-worth through others alone; it needs to come from within.

You're here to discover your own values, abilities and talents; to depend on yourself and establish your self worth through your own efforts, and to enjoy nature, serenity and peace without your innate and often unconscious need to create crises.

In this lifetime you are learning to attune yourself to the quiet rhythms of life, realizing there is a season for everything. Smell the roses and allow things to unfold and grow in their own good time. Find ways to unravel your intensity and build your finances, resources and life slowly but surely over time.

Define your goals based on your own personal value system, and then work towards them in a patient manner. This steady approach to life will help you to achieve happiness and inner balance.

This description also applies if you have your North Node in the 2nd house.

North Node in Gemini/South Node in Sagittarius

You came into this life with a strong intuition and can immediately see what should be done in a situation. However, in this life you are also here to gather facts and knowledge to support your intuition, rather than relying solely on what you feel and know to be true. In this way you can convince others more easily rather than sounding dogmatic. You are born to be a communicator and can be a brilliant teacher and mentor of others as long as you take the time to gather all the facts.

You have a tendency to hold strong beliefs and opinions, to be self-righteous and run roughshod over others' feelings, rushing through life with excess nervous energy. You are here to develop tact and diplomacy. You want to have meaningful and intelligent exchanges with others and want to teach others as well. In order to succeed you need to listen to others so you can discover the value of true communication and avoid being dogmatic.

You can easily crack under imagined pressures, and are too often in a hurry for fear that your freedom will be curtailed if you stop long enough to gather facts and consider the details. Learning to slow down and be sensitive to what others are saying, will release you from some of your nervous tension. This will help you to achieve happiness and inner balance.

This description also applies if you have your North Node in the 3rd house.

North Node in Cancer/South Node in Capricorn
Above all, you need to be in control. From an early age, you took your responsibilities seriously and a strong, innate sense of duty has made you rigid and rather fearful. One fear you have is of being dependent on others. When you release your need to be in control you can then achieve your goals in life.

Let go of a tendency to over-manage yours and other people's lives, relax your standards of perfection and achievement, and value your personal achievements.

You need to allow yourself to be vulnerable, exposing your insecurities and needs in a healthy way. It is also important for you to make time for your home and family life because you are overly career-oriented.

By working on your inner foundation, success will ricochet back to you. Spend time in reflection and meditation. By allowing yourself to follow your instincts, rather than be driven by ambitions, you can achieve fulfillment in all areas of life.

This description also applies if you have your North Node in the 4th house.

North Node in Leo/South Node in Aquarius
You have a tendency to rely on others, and come across as impersonal or distant. You're fearful of being the center of attention and standing out as an individual. You tend to fall back on peers at the expense of your own individuality.

Stop worrying about impressing others. Instead, strike out fearlessly on your own creative path. Make a conscious effort to deal with others in a more personal and loving manner rather than taking a purely intellectual approach which detaches you from your feelings.

You can alienate others when you over-emphasize equality. While this is a good thing, you can do it to the point that you don't acknowledge others' uniqueness. You can too easily lose touch with your own heart by rationalizing. You can become overly involved with others' problems at the expense of your inner needs for attention.

You are learning to take personal risks and to find self-confidence. You are learning to stand out as an individual of confidence and leadership. You find fulfillment in pursuing your own dreams rather than in seeking the spotlight.

This description also applies if you have your North Node in the 5th house.

North Node in Virgo/South Node in Pisces

You avoid dealing with the details and practicalities of everyday life, formulating clear goals, and put too much faith in a grand plan.

You need to develop healthy routines and schedules or you will have vague worries and anxieties. Winging life is fine, but without clear goals and orderliness, you will feel you're not in control.

You have great compassion for others. Taken too far, however, you risk being used. Your goal is to establish limits for others and yourself; to develop a more focused mind and systems that will help you to be more productive and pay attention to deadlines, details, and rules that will enrich your life. By structuring things in this way, you will achieve your dreams.

You are here learning discernment and discrimination and your goal is Service in the highest sense of the word.

This description also applies if you have your North Node in the 6th house.

North Node in Libra/South Node in Aries

You have opposite lessons to a person with the North Node in Aries. You have a tendency to rely on yourself so much that you alienate others; you are competitive, with a me-first attitude. You take things personally and are impatient and impulsive. You need to sensitize yourself to the needs of others, learning tact and cooperation. Put yourself in another's shoes. You tend to go it alone, passing up opportunities for growth because you are too focused on survival.

You are afraid of the demands that a partner might put on you, and don't look for feedback, preferring to act in the moment following your own hunches and impulses. The more you push for yourself alone, the more you will be blocked. Your instincts are overloaded and lacking in perspective. Acting upon them may bring strife until you learn to consider the other side. Through partnership and cooperation you will attain the inner balance necessary for you to achieve your goals.

This description also applies if you have your North Node in the 7th house.

North Node in Scorpio/South Node in Taurus

You have opposite lessons to a person with the North Node in Taurus. You came into this life with a strong grasp of reality. You are grounded and self reliant with a sense of your own worth and talents, all of which are good. However, this surety can make you overly set in your ways. You cling on to your possessions as security blankets because you are overly focused on material and emotional security.

In order to learn the lessons of this lifetime, you need to loosen the grasp on things and people and open up to your soul's need for intensity, change and transformation from the material to the psychic and spiritual realms.

You experience difficulties in relationships because you are so strongly centered in your own values that you may be blind to the values of others. You know how to support yourself and look after your needs but you are here to learn about sharing at a deep level. This will give you the security you crave.

Because of your practical nature, you may be imprisoned in the safe world of the tried and true and in the world of the senses. You are here to learn to be fearless in confronting change and crisis.

Release yourself from always stubbornly having to do things your own way; take into account other people's values, and this will help you find inner balance and satisfaction.

This description also applies if you have your North Node in the 8th house.

North Node in Sagittarius/South Node in Gemini

You have opposite lessons to a person with the North Node in Gemini. You have come into this with a strong intellect and were attracted to learning and the development of your mind from a young age. At any one time you may read several books at once and be learning several new topics. You love to learn and are strongly aware that there is a fascinating world of knowledge out there.

However, because of this you are overwhelmed by information overload and mentally over-stimulated. The details of everyday life may bog you down. When faced with making decisions, you feel swamped unable to see the right answer in the myriad of possibilities. You are here to develop your higher mind, your intuition. You are here to gain a vision and a view of the big picture rather than get caught up in all the details.

It is difficult for you to commit to any one opinion or any one path in life as you see so many possibilities. You must develop your spiritual self, trust your inner guide and enjoy the thrill of following a hunch.

Your decisions will lead you astray if you rely on facts alone. Open yourself up to believe in something that doesn't necessarily make sense. If you do this you will feel happier and freer from stress and doubt.

This description also applies if you have your North Node in the 9th house.

North Node in Capricorn/South Node in Cancer
You have opposite lessons to a person with the North Node in Cancer. You are overly attached to your childhood and past, are dependent on others and avoid accepting responsibility. You fear rejection and may spend too much time and energy on emotional problems.

You need to take charge of your life and accept responsibility. You may blame your past or focus on insecurities and difficulties instead of depending on yourself. Security is very important but it will only come when you carve out a responsible life. You are more aware of your emotions than most but in order to grow you must learn to strike a balance between sensitivity and responsibility. Recognition will come to you as soon as you let go of the past.

You are here to define goals and a mature approach to life; and to achieve the financial and emotional security you crave.

This description also applies if you have your North Node in the 10th house.

North Node in Aquarius/South Node in Leo
You have opposite lessons to a person with the North Node in Leo. Some of your life lessons are to avoid becoming too focused on getting what you want, or on the drama of life and romance. With your Leo south node you were born to lead as a uniquely creative person who stands out in the crowd. You are now here to focus on being objective, impartial, rational and logical. The more you strive towards this scientific frame of mind, the more successful you will be. You have an affinity for the new sciences and also for astrology.

You no longer have to cultivate yourself, as you were born with a highly developed sense of self and confidence. Now you are here to cultivate your ideals, aspirations and close friendships. These will bring you great satisfaction.

One of the ways in which you can improve your relationships is to realize that you are involved with equals. Offer freedom to your partners instead of trying to control them or expecting them to be as you want. You work well in teams and can create and lead a team of equals with everyone having respect for each other. Another thing for you to cultivate is your sensitivity to the needs of others. Let go of the strong desire to get what you want. Satisfaction will come as you find what you need.

You are here to learn to be objective, logical with a scientific approach, and to cultivate ideals and true friendships.

This description also applies if you have your North Node in the 11th house.

North Node in Pisces/South Node in Virgo

You have opposite lessons to a person with the North Node in Virgo. You may be plagued by vague feelings of guilt about under-performing and may lack faith. You need to learn faith in spiritual powers and in the "big picture". Let go of fears that you are not doing enough, love yourself and others and be humble. You are here to move from your active intellect to develop your heart. You are here to develop trust, understanding and compassion. Let go of obsessions with rules, details, and fears of not doing things perfectly. Realize there is a plan that is bigger than you are and you must surrender some of your anxieties to cooperate with this plan. It is only when you do that you will find your pot of gold.

Your spiritual path lies in compassion and in causing things to happen with the sheer power of faith. In fact, in your lifetime, a great secret destiny will be revealed to you.

This description also applies if you have your North Node in the 12th house.

The Part of Fortune

Another astronomical point in your horoscope is the *Part of Fortune*. This is represented as a circle with a cross inside, and is computed from the longitudes of the Sun, Moon and Ascendant. The Part of Fortune represents worldly success and prosperity, and can be indicative of your career or vocation. Its sign and house placement suggest innate abilities and talents that you express naturally.

The Angles of Your Horoscope

In the final part of this Step, we will examine the angles of your horoscope. These are the Ascendant, the IC, the Descendant and the Midheaven. In an Equal House system, these four significant points are respectively the cusps of the 1st, 4th, 7th and 10th houses.

You are at the center of your horoscope. The top of the chart is directly above your head and is known as the *MC* (*medium coeli*, Latin for *"middle of the heavens"*) or *Midheaven*. The bottom is known as the *IC* or *imum coeli* (Latin for *"bottom of the sky"*). This is beneath and on the other side of earth. At left is the Ascendant or rising sign and right is the Descendant or cusp of your 7th house.

Whereas the Ascendant represents the way you appear to the world, your Descendant reflects your relationships and what you project onto others. It also shows what you need and want from others and what you are willing to take from them. Your Midheaven represents your public persona. It's different from your Ascendant in that it's not the way you are initially perceived but more about your career and social standing. Your IC is the point of your horoscope that reflects your approach to attaining security.

Look at your horoscope now and see what planets you have, if any, within ten degrees of these four angles. Planets here affect your public visibility and their effect is intensified. The closer a planet is to one of the angles, the stronger the effect. Famous, high-profile people often have three or more planets close to the angles. If you have planets near your angles, look at the planets in question. Planets here indicate how others view you. If you have Venus near an angle, you are viewed as a diplomat, a harmonizer, an attractive and artistic person. If you have Mercury on your Midheaven, you would be viewed as a communicator. If you have planets near your Ascendant, you are overpowering, right out in front, ready to be tripped over.

I have a friend with Pluto there and she comes across as a powerhouse, broody and action-packed. You can't hide away your Ascendant; it's very visible, especially if you have a planet that tends to stick out anyway, like Uranus. In that case you would be viewed as eccentric. I recently spoke to the mother of a son with Uranus on his Ascendant. Apparently, this young man had nose rings and body piercings but with his Capricorn Sun was as responsible and disciplined as they come. Never be fooled by appearances; astrology is a tool to help you look beneath the surface.

I'm going to end this Step with an allegory to clarify the difference between the angles.

Allegory about The Angles

Imagine you're in London looking down Pall Mall at Buckingham Palace. First you see the flagstaff with the Union Jack flying in the breeze. This is an emblem that reveals the identity of the reigning monarch of the United Kingdom to all approaching. This flag is similar to your point in the horoscope called the Midheaven, which reflects your public reputation. It tells others something about you when they're approaching from a distance.

You continue down Pall Mall and are soon able to check out the palace from behind the iron railings. You see its size, the grounds and the Royal Guards. The exterior gives you a first impression before you go inside. You are impressed with the tradition and have already gained an impression of the palace. The exterior is analogous to your Ascendant. This is the part of you that people see when they're getting to know you.

The image you had of the palace before you entered may be different from what's inside. From the outside the palace didn't seem welcoming with its iron railings and guards. Upon entering, however, it is very different with its spectacular Marble Hallway, Green Room, Music Room,

Ballroom, Garter Throne Room, State Dining Room and more. Each of these rooms can be likened to the houses in your horoscope.

If you have been invited to Buckingham Place in order to receive an honor from Her Majesty the Queen, you will meet the Queen and her entourage. These could include her charming Private Secretary, her Press Secretary, her gracious Lady-in-Waiting and brave Equerry. These characters are like the planets in your horoscope, each with their colorful personalities and different roles.

Step 2 Jargon

Dual signs	Signs of the zodiac ruled by two planets, i.e. Scorpio, Sagittarius and Pisces
MC or *Midheaven*	The top of your horoscope; indicates your public persona
IC	The bottom of your horoscope; indicates your approach to finding security
Descendant	Cusp of your 7th house opposite your Ascendant. Your relationships
Sun sign	The sign of the zodiac the Sun was in when you were born
Moon sign	The sign of the zodiac the Moon was in when you were born
Nodes of the Moon	These astronomical points, the *north node* and the *south node*, also known as the dragon's head and tail, are not planets but sensitive points on the *ecliptic*
The Part of Fortune	It is a primary indicator of prosperity and it created from the longitudes of the Sun, Moon and Ascendan
Ecliptic	The ecliptic is the apparent path of the Sun and planets through the heavens as seen from the Earth

Step 2 Exercises

- Learn the above jargon.
- Make a note of your Moon sign and Sun sign; their qualities according to the signs of the zodiac, the elements and modalities. Write down their qualities and combine the two.
- Make a note of your Ascendant and its qualities according to the sign of the zodiac, the element and modality. Write down how you might use this as a mask.
- Combine your Moon sign, Sun sign and Ascendant and how these operate in your life.
- Make a note of your descendant, MC and IC and their qualities, elements and modalities. Write down how others might see you and also your security needs based on this.
- Note your North Node and South Node and write down how these work in your life.

STEP 3

THE PLANETS: ARE YOU A MERCURIAL TYPE IN A SATURNIAN WORLD?

Envision the extraordinary brilliance and effects of the light in sun and moon and stars, in the dark shades of a glade, in the colors and scents of flowers. Then there is the grandeur of the spectacle of the sea as it slips on and off its many colors like robes. Look at the heavens and the earth... It was you, O Lord, who created them. – Augustine

My best friend at school for about a year was so confident, funny and pretty that she drew every boy within a five-mile radius into her orbit. Suzanna made me laugh because she was not only bright but she also had an extremely caustic wit. She could sum people up in the wink of an eye and deliver what was tantamount to verbal abuse in such a charming manner that even the recipients of her abuse felt honored to be singled out. You may not be surprised to hear she was a Scorpio sun with the moon in Libra and Leo rising; a veritable bundle of magnetic attraction.

I did find out, six months into our friendship, that Suzanna was not as she appeared. She had learned to act a part and she did it remarkably well. Inside, she was seething with complexes and anxieties. Around that time (we were both fourteen), I began studying astrology and used poor Suzanna as my first human guinea pig. Although we drifted apart after school, she has remained to this day a fascinating case study. I would like to thank her for illustrating to me so vividly that even though the Sun, Moon and Ascendant are vitally important parts of your horoscope, they are still only a small part of the picture.

Welcome to the role of the celestial ambassadors, the planets who bring each of us a cornucopia of gifts, talents and challenges. In Suzanna's case, the challenges represented by the planets proved to be too great. It took the poor girl years of therapy to work through her difficulties. Had I met Suzanna twenty years later, I could have been a better friend; I would have used my knowledge of the planets to help her in a more compassionate way.

In this Step we are going to focus on the ten planets – the Sun, Moon, Mercury, Venus, Mars, Jupiter, Saturn, Uranus, Neptune and Pluto. The planets are always listed in their order of speed and distance from the Sun, with the fastest moving, the Moon, being first. The ancient astrologers only used seven planets because what are now known as the outer planets, Uranus, Neptune and Pluto, were then undiscovered. Uranus was discovered in 1781, Neptune in 1846 and Pluto in 1930.

As you may remember from Step 1, the Sun and Moon, Mercury, Venus and Mars are the *personal planets* and these have a more direct effect on your personal life. If gentle Pisces falls on the cusp of your 7th house of relationships, for example, you will relate to others in a warm, compassionate way and will seek sensitive, sweet and spiritual types of relationships.

Jupiter and Saturn come next. Jupiter's transit through all twelve signs of the zodiac takes an average of twelve years and slower moving Saturn takes twenty-eight years. Transits of these planets have a profound effect; Jupiter brings us our good karma and Saturn a reality check.

Next are Uranus, Neptune and Pluto. These *outer planets* have a generational effect. As each planet takes several years to transit a sign, many people born in the same generation have these planets in the same sign. Uranus spends on average seven years transiting a sign, Neptune, fourteen years and Pluto, up to thirty years. These planets move so slowly that they affect change in our lives in a profound way. They also bring about global changes, such as trends and fashions, as well as changes of consciousness and natural disasters.

Even astronomers agree that defining a planet is tricky. To think of a planet as just a lump of rock or a swirling disc of gas and dust left after the formation of a star leaves much to be desired. If this was the case, how could the energies from the planets affect us in the way they do? My own belief, based on over thirty years of research into metaphysics and the spiritual sciences, is that the planets are highly advanced living beings, including our own beautiful Earth. The planets work in divine symphony to bring great God-given energies throughout the solar system to benefit all life and aid in the cosmic process of evolution. We, as sparks of the divine, are here learning lessons on the material plane gradually unfolding more of our divine nature.

It may all sound a bit "cosmic" and out of your control but remember your life is like a play and the planets represent the actors in your personal drama. Actors will only improvise if you haven't provided them with a script and so it is with the planets. The energies provided by the planets are like tools for you to use, not out-of-control bundles of energy waiting to wreak havoc.

The influence of the planets is always positive. It's up to you how you use this influence. If you have your planet of relationships, Venus, in difficult aspect to limiting Saturn, you can cry all you want at how unfair it is that all your relationships are such a burden. However, Saturn gives us the energy of structure and work, so if you're prepared to work at them you can succeed in having good, healthy relationships.

On this stage of life represented by your horoscope, let's assign roles to each planet and see how these cosmic players perform.

The Sun

The Sun is the leading actor, the starring role and the one who produces the play. It rules the sign of Leo. You may dream and hope to be a thousand things according to your Moon sign and the other planets, but the Sun is what you are. It's your vitality and fuel; without the life-giving Sun, you wouldn't be alive.

When you consciously inhabit your Sun sign you gain power. How do you do that? If you have the Sun in Leo, you should consciously seek center stage, take charge, be bold, honorable and magnanimous. Not in an arrogant way but in a confident way, sure of your own power. If you're a Cancer, seek to nurture not just your family but the whole world, wherever your love is needed and wherever you feel injustice. If you're an Aquarian, create teams, espouse social causes and join groups dedicated to peace.

If you use the power bestowed by your Sun sign, you then become like a magnet attracting the energies of the planets like iron filings. You can use these like ambassadors, sending them out on missions. Send out your ambassador, Mercury, when it is time to talk. Send diplomatic Venus, when attending an important dinner party. Use powerhouse Mars when action is needed. It may sound strange to act in this way, but it's about playing the game of life with more awareness of the power you have at your disposal. It's about becoming more conscious of who you are.

When you are "acting out" your Sun, you are purposeful, directed, proud, and creative. On the negative side, you can be haughty, overly willful, self-centered, and judgmental.

The Moon

The Sun's co-star is the Moon, the ruler of Cancer. While the Sun is your adult, the Moon is your inner child and mother. It reflects your relationship with your Mom and/or daughter and is your feelings, needs, habits and unconscious reactions. While it's important to center in your Sun sign, you can't afford to ignore your Moon's needs. If you do, you'll just keep pushing your feelings and insecurities under the carpet and they will fester and ultimately build to a crisis point.

For example, if you have a Libran Moon, you have a strong innate sense of justice. When life all around you is unfair you can choose to ignore the injustice and bury your head in the sand. However, if you do that long enough, it will backfire. Although, ultimately, we don't have power over others we do have the power to change ourselves. If you see no justice perhaps it's because you are supposed to be bringing justice. If you act in the light of this feeling, you are satisfying your Moon's needs and you will feel happier about yourself.

While the Sun acts, the Moon reacts. How do you instinctively react to problems? How do things make you feel? What do you need to be secure? The Moon infuses you with memories from the past while the Sun reflects the here and now. For true happiness neither give your Moon too much nor too little importance.

Mercury

Mercury is the messenger of the Gods, the ruler of Gemini and Virgo. It is the planet of day-to-day expression. *"What shall I buy at the store? What time is my appointment with the dentist? Should I cook my boyfriend dinner or wait for him to take me out?"* Mercury does the talking and rules your thought processes. It is the light in your eye, your intelligence and your ideas. It is unemotional and curious. The sign your Mercury is in and the aspects it makes to the other planets, shows how neat your handwriting is and what chance you have to become an author.

Our modern world is mercurial, as communication is speedy and instantaneous. The influence of Mercury (the higher aspect of Mercury is Hermes, the messenger and also the alchemist) is felt more than ever before, bringing people and countries together through global telephone networks and the Internet. People make connections through e-mails and find information instantly through Google. The Mercurial influence is friendly, but it doesn't make a deep connection. Think of the nature of e-mails and you will understand the type of connection Mercury makes.

Mercury also represents your coordination. If you have a strong Mercury, you may well be good at dancing and movement. Two great dancers were the late Fred Astaire and Michael Jackson; both of them have Mercury close to charming Venus bringing ease and harmony to their skilful dance routines.

When you are "acting out" your Mercury, you are inquisitive, curious, communicative and versatile. On the negative side, you can be high-strung, nervous, nit-picky and indecisive.

Venus

Venus is the ruler of Taurus and Libra. I believe we receive messages from everyday symbols. Have you noticed a time in your life when you kept seeing pink roses or hearts or crosses? These types of "coincidences" reinforce Jung's concept of synchronicity. However, I don't believe that coincidences actually exist but instead it is the meaning of the symbols communicating with us. When my mother died I was strongly impressed (and also told by my psychic cousin) that she would send me pink roses as a sign. From that moment until this day, at difficult or important times in my life, I receive pink roses from every corner. Cards, flowers, advertisements or plants keep pouring in to comfort and help me. Prior to my mother's passing at another extremely difficult time in my life I found myself surrounded by hearts, in every shape and form. I even had a physical manifestation of a small red heart appear to me one day in my bedroom, but that is another story that appears on my website www.chrissieblaze.com.

I am not sure what this has to do with Venus, except that pink roses and hearts are both associated with love and love can perform miracles. Venus is that miracle-making part of your horoscope if you allow it to be. Like all the planets, you can choose to use the lower manifestation of the energy or its higher, more mystical, alchemical version.

Venus operates like a refined version of your Moon and it rules the arts. It represents two main areas of life: love and your value system. It affects how you handle the things you value which include money, possessions, photographs, paintings, music, friendships or loved ones.

Venus rules your sentiments and your ability to give and receive love, to appreciate and be appreciated. It is your charm factor (or not), your grace and beauty; the ability to get along with others in relationships and social graces. Where it is in your horoscope is your *Attraction Principle*; your ability to attract things and people and your artistic nature. Venus energy is harmonious, and this is why people with Venus prominent are often peace-makers. In Mahatma Gandhi's horoscope, his two most prominent planets were Uranus, the awakener, and Venus, the peace-maker.

When you are "acting out" your Venus, you compromise, make peace, are forgiving and compassionate, and act with taste. On the negative side, you can be self-indulgent, self-centered, vain and superficial.

Mars

Mars is the planet of energy, action, and desire. It is the ruler of Aries and the co-ruler of Scorpio. It represents action and is the way you assert yourself. It is what fires you up, what gets you out of bed in the morning and what lights your fire. It is also your survival instinct. On a physical level, whereas Venus rules romantic attraction, Mars is associated with sexual attraction. Mars shows how you apply your drives, express your enthusiasm and the types of experiences you seek.

People sometimes dismiss Mars as being assertive and bloody minded. You might not like those Martian types of people who look you straight in the eye, daring you to mess with them but you secretly have to admit you respect their strength. Like one of my television heroes, Jack Bauer, in the action-packed series 24, you can take everything away from him, mock him and torture him and still he has something you don't even dare to embrace. Look at the power of Mars in your horoscope and you can see how likely you are to run into a burning building to save a stranger.

Never underestimate this planet, or you could end up like a blob of gello on the kitchen floor, waiting to be squished. Without Mars you would never get out of bed in the morning. It is a vital energy that drives you to build and to achieve your goals. Understand its power of raw energy, embrace it, wield it and you too can conquer fear.

When you act out your Mars in a positive way, you are assertive, directed, forthright and adventurous. On the negative side, you are impulsive, rash, impatient, aggressive and forceful.

Jupiter

Jupiter is the planet of good fortune and abundance and the ruler of Sagittarius. Jupiter seeks insight through knowledge. Some of this planet's keywords include tolerance, morality, gratitude, hope, honor, the law, religion and philosophy. Jupiter represents the luck or good karma factor in your horoscope. It is your generosity and it also represents what you take for granted. A person with Jupiter in their 5th house of romance is bound to be lucky in love.

I recently received an e-mail from a desperate family. An elderly aunt, who knew a little about astrology, saw Jupiter transits in her chart and thought she was about to win the lottery. She was having a great time contacting scam merchants all over the world and spending a small fortune trying to make this happen! The lady was on a roll, thinking big in typical Jupiterean fashion. Her family was scared this dear lady would blow her savings and not have anything to leave them in her Will! This lady was definitely displaying some of the effects of a Jupiter transit – an urge to expand her life, blind optimism and overspending – and a sense of fun while doing it.

Jupiter is associated with humor and good will. The more negative manifestations of Jupiter include excess and overindulgence. Jupiter also represents things that bring abundance, joy and expansion– such as music, art, color and sound.

Saturn

Saturn is the great teacher, the ruler of Capricorn and the co-ruler of Aquarius. This wonderful yet serious planet of reality checks and bound-aries is associated with restrictions and limitations. While Jupiter expands, Saturn constricts. Saturn brings structure and meaning to your world and if used wisely helps you to build your dreams on firm founda-tions. Saturn reminds you of responsibilities and brings definition. Saturn makes you aware of the need for self-control, maturity and wisdom.

Why should a great teacher bring limitation? Allow me to explain how it works. If you act out of tune with the universal flow of life that is geared towards evolution and love, Saturn's energies will block you. If you go selfishly towards what you want, ignoring the needs of others, Saturn will stop you. If your choices become purely self-centered based on what you *want* rather than what you really *need*, Saturn will limit your life in some way so that you wake up. This limitation can come through ill health, an authority figure or some external discipline. Saturn is teaching us to operate from a less self-centered place.

Saturn is associated with authority figures and traditional values. In childhood, the discipline, rules and regulations imposed by parents, teachers and other authority figures were not always pleasant but they helped us to learn. Similarly, Saturn's energies help us to learn through discipline.

Uranus

The energies of Uranus are electric and crammed with change. Uranus is forward-looking, original and rules the "genius" factor. It gives the ability to tap the higher intuition and aspects of mind. This unpredictable planet is the ruler of Aquarius, together with Saturn. Uranus is associated with technology, innovation, discovery, and all that is progressive. This Aquarian Age is ruled by both the tradition and discipline of Saturn and the progressiveness of Uranus.

A typical Uranian type of personality was Nikola Tesla who had Uranus rising when he was born within one degree of his Ascendant. Tesla invented the alternating-current induction motor; a device that was previously considered to be impossible to design. Until Tesla had decided to confront this supposedly unsolvable problem, direct current was considered to be the only way to distribute electricity. Tesla's invention revolutionized the modern use and distribution of electricity and enabled cities to receive a safe, reliable form of electrical current. This awesome feat was achieved on a large scale for the first time with his lighting of the 1893 Chicago World Columbian Exposition. Tesla was indeed a genius.

On the up side, Uranus is associated with enlightenment, progressiveness, objectivity, and ingenuity. It's where we go against tradition or authority that is outworn and no longer serves the good of the whole. Uranus represents the spark of intuition that spurs invention or investigation. Negative expression of Uranus is a rebel without a cause and irresponsibility.

Neptune

Neptune is the planet of inspiration, dreams, psychic receptivity, illusion and confusion. Neptune is the sensitive poet and mystic, and the ruler of Pisces.

The Neptune-ruled person strives for communion, the ecstasy of never having to leave her lover's or her mother's arms. The god, Neptune, rules the ocean and it is this type of oceanic oneness, this blissful state that Neptunian-type personalities crave.

I have a prominent Neptune in my horoscope. My mother told me that when I went to the seaside as a small child I would wobble into the water in my romper suit and white sun hat and sit there motionless for hours at a time. I don't remember the experience in great detail but I do remember how happy I felt. I was definitely a water-baby. I proudly told my frantic parents who had found me after being submerged in a swimming pool for several minutes that I had been breathing underwater. To this day, I'm sure I did. I can remember the feeling of oneness. I had a great love for water, and swimming was second-nature to me. Unfortunately, I contracted skin allergies due to chlorine and polluted seawater and now my water exploits are few and far between. However, I later took up the other Neptunian pursuit of mysticism like a psychic duck to water.

Neptune is associated with intuition, subtlety and spiritual enlightenment. It is the planet of mercy and compassion. The more negative manifestations of Neptune include deception, trickery, deceit, guilt and addiction.

Pluto

I have a lot to say about Pluto, which was demoted from its lofty planetary status on the same day that an important fourteen-year cycle started – August 23, 2006. Showing how out of tune the astronomers were, this day of Pluto's demotion was, astrologically-speaking, an important turning point in Pluto's influence. It's a shame that astronomers and astrologers can't get along like they used to because they could help each other to understand the universe. I predict that astrology and astronomy will become twin sciences again as they used to be. The good news is despite what labels are slapped on or taken off Pluto they have absolutely no effect on its powers.

How does Pluto, the ruler of Scorpio, work in your horoscope? Its intense energies are transformative. It operates rather like an atom bomb that disturbs and brings things to the surface; or like a spotlight shining on our fears and urging us to face them honestly. Propaganda, falseness, hypocrisy and weakness are not of Pluto's alchemical realm. Pluto's quest is to transmute the base metal of your lower nature into the gold of your higher nature through change.

Where you find Pluto in your horoscope is where you find endings and new beginnings, spiritual growth and rebirth. When you come through a Pluto transit you are changed forever but during the process you don't realize what's going on. If you refuse to accept your deepest soul needs to change, you will have it painfully thrust upon you. There is actually nothing to fear; you just have to surrender to the mysterious process of this complete transformation. Just think of the butterfly's painful emergence from the chrysalis. That is what's happening in human terms.

Because it's a slow-moving planet, remaining up to thirty years in each Sign, it affects an entire generation. It also rules mass movements and great political and social changes. Astrologers talk about the Pluto in Leo generation or the current Pluto in Sagittarius generation.

The Movement of the Planets

Even the way the planets move in the Cosmos is significant in astrology. There are three movements of the planets – stationary, direct or *retrograde*. A stationary brings with it highly-focused energy. Direct planets also exert considerable influence. It is the retrograde planets that mix things up. By appearing to move backward, these planets generate a diffused and unfocused energy. However, they also can help you to "think outside the box." If you have a little "R" after a planetary symbol, it means it is retrograde. The retrograde planet that affects us most is Mercury Retrograde and if you want to know more about this fascinating little planet you can read my book: *Mercury Retrograde: Your Survival Guide to Astrology's Most Precarious Time of Year* by O Books, 2008.

Planets in the Signs of the Zodiac

You know by now that the planets are colored by the signs of the zodiac and the houses they are in. If you have the Sun in Aquarius you are a strong character, forthright and idealistic and likely to espouse causes. However, when you relate to someone at a party you may come across in an entirely different way. Why is this? In social settings, you may operate more through your Venus, the social planet. Your Venus is not necessarily in the same sign as your bold Aquarius Sun, but perhaps in sensitive Pisces. In this case your bold Aquarian nature is modified by sweet, shy Pisces when meeting people for the first time. Take a look at your horoscope now and see which sign your Venus is in. Refer back to Step 1 for the main characteristics of that sign.

Now look at your Mars as you read this next example. You are on the football field and playing tough. As a female you can take on any man and kick as good as you get. What's going on here? When you are physically active you are using the energy of the planet Mars and in this example you have Mars in scrappy Aries. This shows another side of your complex personality. Think about how your Mars might act by looking at the sign it is in.

Are you beginning to see how this works? You analyze each planet in the different signs and also where they are physically located in the twelve houses. Remember, your horoscope is a whole unit not a bunch of disconnected pieces, just as a person is not simply a collection arms, legs and internal organs. Your horoscope is made up of all these bits and pieces and from these, the whole you emerges. Astrology is like any language; first you learn the words, the pronunciation and the grammar and then suddenly it all makes sense!

We've looked at the Sun and the Moon and how their effect is modified by the sign they're in. Now let's look at the other planets and how they fare in the different signs. You can use these examples to see how to analyze the planets in your horoscope. As you will see, you combine the nature of the planet with the nature of the sign it's in.

Mercury in the Signs

First ask yourself what role Mercury plays in your horoscope? It is the light in your eye, your communicator; it rules your concrete mind, your thought processes, ideas, movement, humor and dexterity.

If you have Mercury in the fixed fire sign of Leo your thought processes and expression will be Leo-like in nature. This means you will tend to communicate in the vivid, dramatic and opinionated manner of a Leo. You like to dance and be noticed, will weave a dramatic story even if all the facts aren't accurate.

If you have Mercury in Sagittarius, you will be optimistic, enthusiastic, honest, philosophical and well-meaning in your speech. Since Sagittarius is intuitive and straight like an arrow, your communication style is forthright and to the point. You will enjoy learning as part of your eternal quest for truth.

If you have Mercury in Libra, you are a good negotiator or mediator. You like fairness and can see both sides of an argument. You are charming and socially active. Because you can see both sides, you are also indecisive.

Mercury in Scorpio would brood over matters, detective-like. Ruled by Pluto, Scorpio wants to get to the bottom of things, so having Mercury there makes a good researcher. Fascinated with subjects like death, birth, sexuality, the occult and healing, you would have a deep, perceptive mind and could be manipulative.

When analyzing Mercury you should also take your Sun sign into account as Mercury never strays very far from the Sun. Mercury will always be either in the same sign or the previous sign to your Sun. I have Mercury in stodgy Taurus but Sun in the previous sign, progressive Aries. This combination is frustrating since I want to rush in where angels fear to tread but my mind lags behind coming up with reasons why I shouldn't. However, this can also keep me out of trouble. It is also a good combination for putting ideas (Aries) into manifestation (Taurus).

Venus in the Signs

Venus is the Love planet representing personal as well as impersonal love, or compassion. Venus in outspoken Aries activates your affections. Liz Taylor has this placement (and for a further layer of planetary influence, her Venus sits close to Uranus, the planet of unexpected change), and so also did the sex sirens, Marilyn Monroe and Jean Harlow. Venus in Aries people don't like to be bored in relationships; they are fast paced and need constant excitement. If things finally slow down and get too comfortable, they may start looking elsewhere. If you have Venus in Aries, don't ruin a great relationship by straying; instead avoid boredom by giving your love to needy children or the elderly. There is never any reason to be bored in this crazy world.

If you have sociable Venus in clever Gemini you are charming with clever dialogue and wit. You would probably never fall in love with a silent person and they would be even more tongue-tied with you around. You have to talk well, intelligently and a lot. This placement of Venus gives a tendency to want more than one love relationship at a time as Gemini likes variety. You can avoid that by becoming a teacher so you can then spread your love every day in the classroom.

With Venus in the fixed water sign of Scorpio you are possessive, obsessive and intense towards lovers or mates. You don't just want a casual, friendly type of relationship like Venus in Gemini; you want something deep, close and very real. You will be a loyal friend but not a half-hearted one. Relationships are seldom light and breezy; you may sometimes love your beloved and friends with all your heart and at other times almost despise them. You are passionate in your feelings, whether they are feelings of love or jealousy. Since Scorpio is also the sign of the "underworld" at some point in your life you may be attracted to shady people. Ironically, you can come out of it renewed like the mythical Phoenix rising out of its own ashes.

Venus in watery Pisces is a romantic combination. You see the beauty in everyone and everything. Venus in Pisces indicates you're a person of unconditional love, sensitivity, romance and empathy. You are naturally giving and want to help those less fortunate but because of your kind nature you may suffer abuse from others. You are spiritually inclined, artistically gifted and naturally psychic. You can sense what the other person is feeling and thinking, and words are unnecessary. If other people are mean to you, it's important to recharge your batteries and defend yourself with spiritual armor.

Mars in the Signs

The power of Mars is what you use when you kick a football or speak out in defense of yourself or another. The energy of Mars in Cancer is expressed emotionally and so this indicates a person of strong but sensitive emotions with a desire to nurture and be nurtured.

One example was the late Sugar Ray Robinson, one of the greatest boxers ever. Sugar Ray had Mars in Cancer and he wasn't the only boxing champion with this placement. He fought with his instincts, in the way Mars in Cancer can, and he won.

If you live with someone who has this placement of Mars keep him busy around the house (Cancer rules the home). As long as he has a constructive outlet for his super-sensitive emotions, the chance of arguments will be minimized.

If you have Mars in Libra you may have the maddening trait of fighting on both sides. Like Mars in Cancer, Mars is also supposed to be weak in this sign. It isn't weak; it just keeps switching from one point of view to the other. Everything has to be fair and equitable and that can be perceived as weakness. However, they don't hesitate when they see obvious injustice.

The energy expressed by Mars in Sagittarius is in spurts. Like the archer, these people shoot their "energy arrows", then stop and reload. Then the next arrow is shot in another direction that looks more interesting. If you have this placement you tire very easily when forced to do boring work even if you are energetic when you begin. Your interest and enthusiasm for what you are doing is tied into your energy levels. Take long walks if you have a Sagittarius Mars in order to avoid restlessness. What is actually restless is your roving mind.

What about Mars in Aquarius? In Aquarius the aggressive energy of Mars is focused on the intellect. This combination indicates someone with an unpredictable mind and possibly even a touch of genius, as with the chess champion, Bobby Fischer.

Jupiter in the Signs

The planet Jupiter represents your good karma or luck factor. It's your urge to grow and how you learn from your mistakes and how and what you teach others. If you have Jupiter in Cancer you will probably have a nice, large, comforting home. Because Jupiter is expansion and Cancer types like food and drink, it can also indicate a tendency to gain weight.

Jupiter in Sagittarius brings a double-dose of luck, since lucky Jupiter is the ruler of Sagittarius. This can be too much of a good thing and because of this you may take things for granted. I had a client with Jupiter in Sagittarius and she was married and divorced three times. She was an elderly, charming lady from good English stock and she was regarded as rather scandalous because of this. Jupiter brought her many opportunities for marriage but she wasn't prepared to work at them. Jupiter is rather *laissez faire*, easy-come, easy-go in its influence.

Jupiter in Saturnine Capricorn can be fortunate. People with this placement don't have the natural luck factor of a Jupiter in Sagittarius but they know how to save pennies and out of the blue they suddenly have a fortune. I know one person with this placement who inherited a struggling business. Everyone advised him to sell it but with Capricorn determination and hard work within three years he had a thriving business. Jupiter in Capricorn can succeed where others fail.

Saturn in the Signs

While Jupiter is your good karma, Saturn is your Achilles heel. The placement of Saturn in your horoscope is where you have to work to succeed. Things don't just drop into your lap as they do with Jupiter. The good thing about Saturn is that if you do work hard, you become an astronaut or a brain surgeon. With Saturn you can achieve anything you work towards. Note that I didn't say "*anything you believe in.*" This is because Saturn really is about work.

A good thing about Saturn is that it gets better as you get older. If you have a prominent Saturn, as you get older it will help you look and feel younger. If you co-operate with Saturn it really does have the magical power of eternal youth.

Saturn indicates what you need to feel secure. If you have Saturn in Aries it means you have to be able to take initiative and have a free rein. The worst thing you can do to this person is try and control them.

If you have Saturn in Taurus you need security such as a nice home, money in the bank and food on the table. You also need routine and dependable people. I know someone with Saturn in Taurus who has been in the same job, the same marriage and doing the same volunteer work for over thirty years. She is able to put up with things that other people just wouldn't. It's because security and routine is her lifeblood. These are extremely loyal people if not a little dull. If you have this placement, work on artistic achievements, you have an innate artistic ability that needs expression and this will bring joy into your life.

If you have Saturn in Leo the last thing you need to feel safe and secure is routine. You want to be in the spotlight as an actor, a speaker or dancer. Though you may suffer with self-consciousness as a child your innate need is to shine. Through hard work and determination you can become the most self aware person of all. You must work on being respected, loved and admired.

Saturn in Pisces is different again. There is a lot of imagination and psychic ability in this person but when they are young they deny this side of their nature. However, as they mature they can become the renowned psychics and wielders of imagination such as artists, musicians, writers. If you have this, you won't feel safe and secure unless your imagination is active.

Uranus in the Signs

Uranus is the unpredictable revolutionary. It thrives in the midst of change and creates change wherever it finds itself. It rules technology, new science and inventions as well as astrology. As Uranus recently (in cosmic terms) left its own sign of Aquarius in 2004, I predict we will see a renewed interest in astrology and the new sciences over the next twenty years.

The sub-generation born with Uranus in Gemini (1943 to 1949) continues to shock by expressing weird, socially unacceptable ideas. These people fueled the social upheavals of the 1960's and their poster child was John Lennon. He loved to upset apple carts (a favorite past time of Uranus) and bring change through using the wit and cleverness of Gemini. He sums himself up in a typically Uranus in Gemini way when he said: "*I'm not going to change the way I look or the way I feel to conform to anything. I've always been a freak. So I've been a freak all my life and I have to live with that, you know. I'm one of those people."* I don't believe he was a freak but a unique individual.

I want to remind you that I am just picking out one planet in a few signs at random to give you illustrations. You have to examine your whole horoscope before you can say for sure that this person will behave in a certain way. You may have been born at the same time as John Lennon but it doesn't make you John Lennon. You have to see what else is going on in your chart.

Another sub-generation was Uranus in Virgo and many of you reading this may have been born at this time between 1962 and 1968. The planet of radical changes is here in the sign of details and here there was an influence of smallness after the grand gestures of Uranus in Leo. It was during this time the transistor replaced the vacuum tube greatly reducing the size of electrical equipment.

Uranus represents the urge to create a new planetary order based upon equality and cooperation. Recently, Uranus was in its own sign of Aquarius from 1997 to 2004. One way in which this planet of change manifested was through the revolution of the Internet. Computer software is another example of this revolution and now astrology is available to all. Uranus changes things dramatically through sudden upheaval, not slowly and delicately as does Neptune, or profoundly like Pluto. Look at your natal Uranus and see what house it is in. See if you can analyze what this might mean.

Neptune in the Signs

Mystic Neptune represents the sea of vibrations in which we live, known as *the ethers* or *the field.* Neptune is the planet that influences the inner heart of religions (not the outward form, which is Saturn) as well as mysticism, poetry, art and the mass media. This planet makes us feel confused or inspired, or probably both. If you have a strong Neptune and are not inspired, you are probably confused. Neptune gives us vision and the ability to see spirituality in the midst of materialism.

Those born in the generation of Neptune in Virgo have the potential for realizing the higher aspects of health and service on a planetary level. These people may be infused with the vision to make a perfect national health service available to everyone. Because Neptune is other-worldly and absent-minded it is not the planet for accountants!

Neptune in Libra represented another sub-generation and this was my generation born between 1943 and 1956. This was before the wildness and free love of the 1960s and 1970s and was a time period that was all about being normal; it was the birth of suburbia. I remember my parents desperately trying to give my brother and me a "normal" life by working long and hard and saving every penny, so that we didn't have to endure the tremendous suffering and hardship they did during World War II. I wish I had appreciated their sacrifice at the time.

If you were born with Neptune in Libra it's important for you to keep your life on an even keel, to keep up appearances and keep the peace (unless of course you have a prominent Uranus or feisty Mars). Neptune is about illusion as well as inspiration. The illusion is to think that if you don't rock the boat everything will be fine. Ironically, this generation did rock the boat during the riots and demonstrations of the 1960s. Most of us were also born with Pluto in Leo, and that's a whole 'nother story.

Also, Neptune is about romance and Libra is about relationships. We were all seeking blissfully romantic relationships. Many of this generation married and remarried several times, ever seeking the ideal.

Now let's look at a more recent sub-generation from 1984 to 1998 when Neptune transited Capricorn. Neptune is about illusion and dreams but now people were ready to actually accomplish their dreams with practical Capricorn bringing concrete expression and the desire to work. This generation holds great hope for our precarious future on this planet.

You may not relate great art to practical Capricorn, but in previous Neptune in Capricorn periods, art flowered because the artists were now willing to spend the time and effort to create masterpieces instead of just dreaming about them.

Pluto in the Signs

As Pluto moves slowly through the signs, it brings great change, personally as well as globally. Its energies incline us to be obsessive, intense and transformative.

When Pluto transited Cancer this brought a generation obsessed with home and homeland. These folks born between 1914 and 1939 grew up during the Great Depression. Cancer seeks security and this generation was driven by hunger and insecurity. My parents were part of this generation and one of their deepest needs was to have a home and a well-stocked larder and fridge. To this day, my Dad never feels secure unless his towering freezer is bursting at the seams.

You may have been born in the Pluto in Leo generation from 1939 to 1956 and then again between 1957 and 1958 when Pluto returned to Leo. We are obsessed with love, self-expression and creativity. We are the baby boomers and "*Do your own thing*" is our motto. Ours is the first generation that isn't prepared to grow old gracefully because Leo is proud about how they look. As our generation ages we are fanatical about staying young, joining health clubs and there is an enormous surge of interest in plastic surgery. Pluto in Leo will always defy authority, unless they are the authority and, believe me, they want to be.

Pluto was last in Virgo from 1956 to 1971 although as mentioned previously there were two years from 1957 and 1958 when Pluto returned to Leo. By contrast with the Pluto in Leo generation, who rioted on the campus for peace, Pluto in Virgo people are more concerned with work and health. If you were born in this generation, you will probably prefer to be active in the background rather than in the spotlight.

Pluto in Sagittarius is the current generation as I write this book (1995 to 2008) and these youngsters will become obsessed with answering the question "*Why?*" We should thank God when we hear them asking this question and not reply with trite responses. This is the generation of seekers who will want to venture into outer space and meet with extraterrestrials. They will be on a quest for the Holy Grail and will not be satisfied with easy answers to questions. Let's give all our support and wisdom to this generation because we really need their vision to take us into the future.

Look at your horoscope and note the signs of all your planets. Refer back to the meanings of the signs in Step 1. combine the nature of the planet with the sign it's in.

Planets in the Houses

We've looked at how the cosmic players, the planets, clothe themselves in the sparkling, sober or security-conscious disguise of the signs of the zodiac that they're in. The next step is to look at the planets in the houses of your horoscope. Think of how feisty Mars might operate in your 7th house of relationships as opposed to your 4th of home and inner self; or how rebellious, truth-seeking Uranus might fare in your 3rd house of communication or your 11th house of friends and aspirations.

Another thing to note is the quantity of planets in a particular house. If Venus, for example, is the only planet in a particular house you will be able to hear its note loud and clear. It is like listening to someone talk. If there is one person in the room it's easy to hear them. If there are several people talking at once, the loudest voice will predominate. If you have several planets in a house, it is the strongest planet or the planet closest to the cusp that you hear the loudest.

Wherever you see a predominance of planets in a certain house, you see right away that this is a room you like to hang out in. Also, if there is more than one planet in a house, their influences will affect and modify each other. If you look at your Mars and the house it occupies, don't simply assume you are active or impulsive in that area of life. It could also be that Saturn, the planet of restriction, is in the same house. The effect of this would be that Saturn would tend to slam the brakes on your Mars.

You may see some of your houses are empty of planets. Don't be alarmed. In all my astrology classes I have found that this revelation causes consternation and even alarm. "*I have nothing in my relationship house. Does that mean I will never have a relationship?*" My answer is "*Do you really want one?*" Remember the planets bring us energy and focus. If you don't have planets in a house it just means you are not putting as much focus there as you are with other areas of your life. However, no house is empty of influence. Each house is actually connected to a planetary influence whether or not it contains a planet.

Finally, each of the planets exerts its most power over the sign it rules. This is referred to as the *sign of its dignity*. Perhaps the most important planet of all is the one that rules the cusp of your 1st house, your Ascendant. If, for example, you have Virgo as the sign on your Ascendant, Mercury, the ruler of Virgo, exerts a considerable influence over your life.

As with the planets in the different signs, I list below how the planets operate in the different *houses* with several examples of each so that you can use these as guidelines for your own interpretation.

The Sun in the Houses

The Sun is where you develop your character and creativity and so it is where you shine. The Sun in a particular house in your horoscope will light up the activities of that house. If you have your Sun in the 1st house of personality, you are here to express who you are and your life's work is all about self-improvement. When you make such an impact through the sheer weight of your personality, you stand out more than other people. This means you just can't get away with things. If you have the Sun in your 9th house of travel and the higher mind, you're on the move and not happy unless you are traveling through developing your mind or hopping on a plane. You are a broad-minded person with a feeling for the whole. Your job is to see the common thread in all religions, philosophies and then broadcast this thread to others through teaching, writing, publishing or speaking. You seek to understand and are intuitive and on a quest for knowledge.

The Moon in the Houses

The position of the moon indicates your emotional, instinctive responses and how receptive you are. If your Moon is in the 2nd house of values and possessions, you will have a great need for security, a tendency to worry about money and to collect things or remain attached to the past in some way. If your Moon is in the 10th house of career, status, recognition and personal achievement are more important to you than financial security. You are a person who is always busy pursuing your next goal and aiming for the mountain top.

Mercury in the Houses

Quicksilver Mercury is even more so if it is in your 3rd house of communication. If you have Mercury here, you are inquisitive and chatty, with your mind "on" all the time. You are a gatherer of information and ideas. Your attention span is brief and you are easily distracted. If Mercury is in your 11th house of friends and aspirations, you like to share your ideas with friends, and your friends will be lively and intelligent. You have a good understanding of group trends, politics and community affairs. Sharing ideas with groups of people is something you are likely to be involved with. You collaborate well in group efforts or in teams.

Venus in the Houses

Venus is where you want love and harmony and what you value. With Venus in your 4th house of home, you want a beautiful home and you would invest your time and energy into creating this. Also, having close family ties is a major priority for you. If Venus is in your 12th house of spirituality, you may hide your affections or find your feelings difficult to express to those you love. You may be tempted by secret love affairs or fall in love with a person who is unavailable to you. Love and sacrifice often seem to go hand in hand for you. You appreciate the suffering of others and value spirituality, self-sacrifice and a giving attitude.

Mars in the Houses

Mars indicates your desires and instinct to act, as well as what makes you mad. With Mars in your 5th house of creativity and children, you are openly affectionate and enjoy being with children. You shine in sports and are a risk-taker who likes competitive sports and rough-and-tumble activities. You take the initiative in sports and in romance and are ardent in pursuing what you desire. You are driven to excel in all forms of creative expression – theater, arts, writing or crafts. You have an urge to express yourself. If you have Mars in the 8th house of shared resources and transformation you have strong desires. You may not experience a really close relationship until later in life, but when you do it is magical and intense. You have some fears of betrayal and loss, and you meet numerous challenges in pursuit of your goals. Setbacks occur when you're too intent on expressing your own will. You are intense, passionate and psychic. You have a strong urge for integrity and contempt for the superficial.

Jupiter in the Houses

Jupiter is where you seek growth and abundance. It's how you express your generosity and tolerance; how you trust others and improve your life. It is where you look for wisdom and understanding. If you have Jupiter in your 6th house of work and health, a career in one of the service or health occupations is possible. You may find yourself taking care of the needs of others in a generous way. Your urge to expand involves your health, diet and routines. With Jupiter in the 7th house of relationships, you seek growth through relationships. Your partners are Jupiterean types with generous spirits and noble attitudes.

Saturn in the Houses

The 1st house is how you project your personal energies onto others. If you have Saturn here you may have a stern exterior but when you smile you can light up the room, because then your superficial exterior drops and the real you shines out. You are your own worst critic and can be too hard on yourself. Self assertion is a big issue for you and people who are appreciative of you rather than critical help your self-esteem. If you have Saturn in the 8th house, change is a big issue for you. This house is to do with transformation and growth and here Saturn holds you back from changing unless you really work at it. Your best approach is to prepare for imminent change by charting out an action plan. Then you can really benefit, grow and reinvent yourself. Another issue is trust and sharing yourself others at a deep level. You are better in relationship with mature people who love and understand you, despite your fears and anxieties.

Uranus in the Houses

Where Uranus falls in your horoscope is where you are different and where you seek freedom. If it is in your 2nd house of values and possessions, you look at things as a means to an end. You don't want possessions to tie you down but that help you towards your freedom. You value freedom above money. You would probably rather share your money with those less fortunate than horde it for a rainy day. If you have Uranus in your 9th house of the higher mind and travel, you are comfortable with new and radical ideas. You want the freedom to travel and meet new people of every culture and belief. You are not at home with conservative belief systems that stifle free thought. You experience sudden flashes of intuition. These can unsettle you, or help you see the truth and bring illumination or unsettle you.

Neptune in the Houses

Neptune reveals your mystic nature but also where you ignore or avoid harsh reality. If you have Neptune in your 3rd house of the everyday mind, you are a daydreamer and inattention to your surroundings can be a problem. Your mind has a tendency to wander if bored and you do best in the creative, artistic world of imagination. You can be evasive or a psychic, who just seem to know things without being told. If you have Neptune in your 10th house of career, you are driven to put your dreams into action. When young you may be confused about your place in the world. Later you struggle to find ways to express your imagination and ideals in your career. Work that involves compassionate service, such as the ministry, may be your calling. You also have a talent for music, art, film-making or entertainment.

Pluto in the Houses

Pluto represents your subconscious forces and everything that is beneath the surface. It brings us the power to change and transform. If you have Pluto in your 4th house of home and inner self, change comes from deep within you and your inner voice guides you, though sometimes in turbulent ways. You are learning to exert your will in healthy ways so that the power doesn't build up inside you and then erupt like a volcano! You need to step into your own power and allow this to heal you. If you have it in your 5th house of creativity, you live life to the full with passion and joy. You are extremely self-expressive and have a need to prove yourself and for personal recognition. If you have children you may want your children to live your dreams for you, but you have the power to bring change through your own intensely creative efforts.

Look at your horoscope and note which houses each of the planets occupy. Refer back to the meaning of the houses in Step 1.

Step 3 Jargon

Retrograde planets	The apparent backward motion of the planets. The most commonly known is Mercury retrograde
The sign of its dignity	Each of the planets exerts its most power over the sign it rules

Step 3 Exercises

- Learn the above jargon.
- Note the influence and power of each planet and which sign of the zodiac it rules.
- In what order are the planets listed?
- What is the influence of Mercury in our world today? How does its influence manifest?
- What are the three movements of the planets.
- What are the personal (inner) and transpersonal (outer) planets?
- What are the main differences between the personal planets and transpersonal planets?
- Note where each of the planets are in your horoscope and write a brief analysis of each one by sign and house.

STEP 4

PLANETARY ASPECTS: FEEL THE FLOW AND IMPROVE YOUR LIFE

"We could use up two eternities in learning all that is to be learned about our own world... Mathematics alone would occupy me for eight million years." Mark Twain

When you start learning about aspects, you may sympathize with Mark Twain's sentiments on mathematics. The good news with aspects, however, is you can just learn the major ones and still interpret your horoscope accurately. We're going to consider five major aspects. There are a lot more aspects including *semisextiles, quintiles* and *sesquiquadrates* but for simplicity's sake we will study just five of the most powerful ones.

In the previous Step you have seen the graceful dance of your natal planets in the signs and houses around your horoscope. Just as everyone on earth is linked to everyone else, so too are the planets connected. They are linked by virtue of their distance or mathematical angles and these planetary relationships are called *aspects.* These aspects are vital keys to your interpretation and add another layer of understanding.

When planets aspect each other, they are rather like two characters in a dance routine. The type of dance depends on the planets involved and the type of aspect they make. Perhaps their energies blend gracefully and they'll be like Fred Astaire and Ginger Rogers. Perhaps their individual energies will conflict and they'll wind up battling like martial artists in a Kung Fu movie.

These aspects are important because happy Jupiter will not be so happy if it makes a difficult aspect to obsessive Pluto; and play-it-safe Saturn will be much more gregarious if in pleasant aspect to Venus. In other words, the effects of the planets are modified by the aspects they make one with another.

Planetary aspects can override other factors in your horoscope, such as which sign a planet is in. For example, if you have a lack of water in chart but watery planet Neptune is in close aspect to your Moon, you would be a sensitive, feeling type of person, even if you had no planets at all in the element of water.

Unfortunately, planets that modify by aspect contribute to the skepticism of those who know little about astrology. The skeptic may have a Virgo Sun that should be so efficient and organized yet he may also have spaced-out, mystical Neptune in close aspect to his Sun. Try telling this skeptical person that he is always on time and great with filing systems and he probably wouldn't relate to that at all. Understandably, he would have a hard time believing in astrology. So you can see the importance of aspects.

If you have your Moon in Leo in your 4th House you could be little Miss Hostess enjoying glitzy parties. However, with Pluto making a powerful aspect to your Moon, your dinner parties would be few and far between and likely to be serious affairs with powerful, intense guests. Since the 4th house is also your inner self, you would have an intensely brooding nature, powerful and dramatic. If Saturn opposes your Sun you would seem like a Saturnian type even with nothing in Capricorn or any of the Earth signs.

The Major Aspects

The five major aspects are as follows:

Conjunction	☌
Trine	△
Sextile	✳
Square	☐
Opposition	☍

You can see from this list that the conjunction is represented by a circle with a line sticking out of the top right, this is used to indicate planets next to each other. The sextile is like a six-pointed star, the square is a square, the trine is a triangle and the opposition like a dumbbell.

Let's look at the aspects in another way which may help you to understand them better. There are twelve signs of the zodiac and each sign contains 30 degrees. If your Jupiter is at 1 degree Aries and your Mars at 1 degree Cancer, these planets would be three signs (or 90 degrees) apart from each other. This 90 degree separation of the planets makes a mathematical square angle and the aspect of 90 degrees is called a square.

If Mercury is at 15 degrees Libra in your horoscope and Jupiter is at 15 degree Aries, then these planets are exactly opposite each other, or six signs apart. As each sign is 30 degrees, six signs is 180 degrees. This 180 degree aspect is called the opposition and is another dynamic aspect.

Orb of Influence

One annoying thing when you are learning astrology is that, as soon as you understand something, you will find there's an exception. So it is with the aspects. It is rare that the planets are at the exact angular distances listed above. In order to calculate aspects, therefore, astrologers use what is called an *orb of influence* or a set number of degrees within which a specific aspect is effective.

For example, two planets that are 94 degrees apart form a square aspect to each other even though they are not at a precise 90 degree square angle. This would be considered an acceptable orb within which the two planets would influence each other. It's also true that the closer the planets are to each other, the stronger the aspect's energy.

Most astrologers use an orb of up to 8 degrees for major aspects. For minor aspects, an orb of between 1 and 3 degrees is considered reasonable. In other words, if two planets are 98 degrees apart they are considered to be in square aspect. If the two planets are 99 degrees apart, however, (outside the 8 degree orb of influence) they would not usually

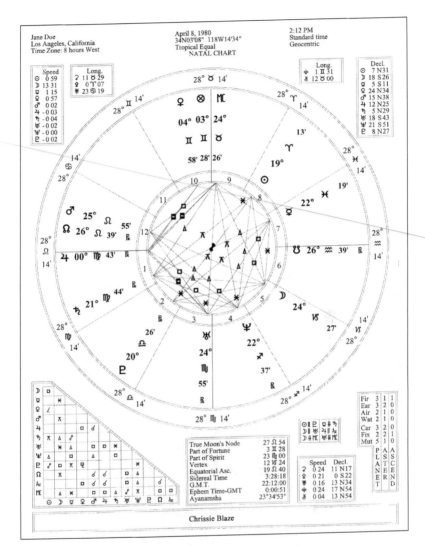

Horoscope Showing The Aspects

be considered to be in aspect to each other.

Now look at the aspects in your own horoscope. Aspects are usually indicated by lines inside the circle of your horoscope that link the planets together. With most horoscopes these aspects are also listed in a chart or grid near the bottom of the chart wheel. If you don't see a grid, you can calculate the aspects yourself by counting the distance from one planet to another. If Mars is at 6 degrees Aries and Jupiter is 6 degrees Gemini, these planets are two signs away from each other. As each sign is thirty degrees, these two planets would be 60 degrees apart, or in sextile aspect. This relationship is expressed as Mars *sextile* Jupiter. If Mars at 6 degrees Aries is also 125 degrees from Saturn, it would be expressed as Mars *trine* Saturn.

When I began studying astrology I had to calculate all aspects by counting the degrees. Although time-consuming, you really learn about the aspects by doing this. I highly recommend you try this ancient counting method with your own horoscope.

Hard and Soft Aspects

Let's analyze the effects of the different aspects. Squares and oppositions are known as hard aspects, because the energy from them represents challenges to be overcome or a balance to be found. Trines and sextiles are considered soft aspects. Their energy is generally harmonious and beneficial. The energy from a conjunction can be positive or negative, depending on the planets involved and other factors in the horoscope.

Remember, your planetary actors are dynamic bundles of energy and when they relate to each other by aspect, this energy is intensified and modified. If, for example, you have the Moon in conjunction aspect to Saturn (expressed as Moon *conjunct* Saturn) your feeling nature (Moon) would not harmonize with your desire for caution and discipline (Saturn). This could manifest as a person who is cautious about letting people get too close too quickly. Finding satisfying solitary activities, such as sports, art or music, would be helpful to their emotional well-being. Let's look at what the different aspects mean.

The Conjunction

The Conjunctions describes planets that are close to each other. They are rather like twins in that their personalities rub off on each other.

Conjunctions add emphasis and there is no mistaking their effects because you really feel them. The energies of the planets in question are united and blended. They are locked closely together in an intimate dance.

The conjunction is easy to spot as it is where two or more planets are right next to each other. Look at your horoscope to see if you have any conjunctions. While conjunctions are often found within the same sign, they sometimes fall within adjacent signs. For example, Mars at 27 degrees Gemini is conjunct Venus at 1 degree in the following sign of Cancer because, although in different signs, they are only 4 degrees apart. Let's look at some examples of conjunctions.

Venus conjunct Saturn: Here the attraction principle meets limitation. You feel you have to make concessions to get what you want. You feel you must adjust to the demands of others to have a satisfactory relationship.

Pluto conjunct Sun: This adds an extra layer of power to your Sun's vitality.

Mars conjunct Moon: You not only have intense feelings but also feel compelled to express them. You are assertive with your feelings.

Saturn conjunct Mars: This is a difficult combination. There is astrological research that indicates that more people with Saturn and Mars conjunctions commit suicide than with other combinations. Please don't worry about this if you have it because I have it also and I am an optimist. I must admit, however, this aspect was difficult when I was young because it is about Mars wanting to assert, combined with Saturn holding you back. I think you can see the potential frustration. On the positive side, however, it gave me discipline and the ability to concentrate.

If you are interpreting a horoscope for someone else, please don't tell them they are suicidal. Aim to be honest and helpful but never dogmatic, realizing your words can hurt or heal. Also, always look at the horoscope as a whole. As far as I am concerned, although I do have Saturn conjunct Mars, I also have an enthusiastic Leo Ascendant and the Sun and Moon in the 9th House, which gives faith and optimism. If in doubt, go for a positive interpretation not a negative one. Inspire people to rise to their best.

Moon conjunct Saturn: The comedian, Ben Stiller, has this conjunction. He is able to channel his emotions (Moon) through his work (Saturn). Also, this conjunction in his 10th house has helped him to make an impact as a public figure. As with many comedians, he appears light-hearted but he is actually a serious man. The Saturn/Moon conjunction also gives a good sense of structure and timing, essential for a comedian.

Mars conjunct Venus: You have a desire for peace and harmony as well as a need to express yourself actively and assertively. This indicates battle as well as bliss, and quite possibly one followed by the other! You seek peace but too much peace would make you feisty. Balance between action and relaxation is helpful for this conjunction.

Stellium

When three or more planets are in conjunction, a *stellium* is formed. This configuration has great energy and makes a strong impact on the sign and house where it resides. See if you have a stellium of planets in your horoscope. If you have a stellium in Aries you are not going to want to sit around feeling harmonious, even if you do have the Sun or Moon in a calmer sign.

The Trine

Trines are approximately four signs apart by virtue of their 120 degree angle or four times 30 degrees. As a result, the planets involved are usually in the same element; fire, earth, air or water. This is partly the reason for the harmony of this aspect. A trine enables an easy flow of energy between two planets; it is favorable, light and joyful in nature. Trines bring pleasure, coupled with an ease in doing things. Like all good things, however, we tend to take them for granted. Trines represent what you have already learned in past lives or your good karma.

People complain about having too many squares and not enough trines but there is a downside to trines. They can indicate laziness or apathy; a desire to accept things as they are and leave it at that. A person who has a lot of trines doesn't push for things and may not achieve as much as someone with more difficult aspects. The beauty of a trine's energy is that it doesn't require much action to be activated. The presence of trines in a horoscope also balances out more difficult aspects, so they are a good thing to have.

Venus trine Saturn: You know how to have responsible and mature relationships. You have good judgment and you understood the need for self-discipline as a key for success from an early age.

Mercury trine Neptune: Nicole Kidman has this aspect, which indicates a gifted artist, actress or photographer. From her work as an actress you can see she has an enthralling style associated with Neptune. Also, she has worked in several movies with mystical or romantic themes.

Grand Trine

A *grand trine* is present when three planets, all in the same element, are approximately 120 degrees from each other. This formation signals great creativity and largesse. A grand trine takes on the characteristics of the element it represents. For example, a grand fire trine has considerable drive while a grand air trine is more intellectual.

The Sextile

The sextile is a beautiful star-like symbol and it is a beautiful thing to have in your chart because it will bring you positive opportunity. If you think of your horoscope as your karma, good and bad, your sextiles represent positive karma. They are similar to trines with talent and ease but a little more 'oomph.' Sextiles cause a lovely flow of energy between two planets and this lack of tension allows you to accomplish things smoothly without too much hard work.

Venus sextile Saturn: You accept responsibilities graciously. You are a good listener who is willing to learn from those with greater experience.

You are easy going and thoughtful

Neptune sextile Pluto: The famous and powerful, Oprah Winfrey, was born with this sextile. This is an indication of a person on a spiritual mission, the seeds of which were planted in past lives.

Mars sextile Sun: One of the US basketball greats, Shaquille O'Neal, has a sextile between warrior Mars to his Sun, an excellent aspect for a champion athlete. Here is a person who can direct his solar willpower with his martial strength in a controlled and effective way.

See if you have any sextiles. Remember, while a sextile will bring you opportunities the onus is still on you to make things happen. A sextile isn't the answer to everything but it's a step in the right direction.

The Square

The essence of the square aspect is dissonance, friction and disruption. Don't cry if you have some; the good news is that squares are character building. You are learning to control the power the square aspects brings. This may be easier said than done but with the energy of the square you have the will to do it. The power doesn't come easily as it does with a trine or sextile but it will come forcefully.

While a square stimulates action, too much tension translates to stress. With squares, you may overdo things and run into obstacles. Squares force us out of complacency and are difficult to manage when we're young. While trines and sextiles are positive, squares and oppositions are our challenges and lessons.

Since squares are roughly three signs apart, they are usually cardinal, fixed or mutable in nature. Two planets approximately 90 degrees apart in the cardinal signs of Aries and Cancer, for example, will form a square aspect. This square operates in these two cardinal signs of action so the aspect would manifest as *friction in action*. Depending on other factors, this would indicate an impulsive, irritable type of person who gets things done.

Planets in square aspect in the fixed signs will operate in a more fixed and measured way. If the square is in mutable signs the effect can be either hard or soft, depending on other factors in the horoscope.

Venus square Saturn: You may have difficulty relating to others or feel left out. You are on the defensive as if you fear the other person will make impossible demands. As a child you may have felt rejected and your most significant lessons are learned in relationships. If you meet people halfway, others will meet you.

Sun square Neptune: Sylvester Stallone has this square which is common in the charts of actors. Neptune represents the world of make believe and imagination, and the square gives power to this world. This also indicates a person who has had to fight for success and interestingly his Rocky films are about a boxer who does just that.

Uranus square Ascendant: The planets also make aspects to the *angles* of your horoscope. Britney Spears has Uranus square her Ascendant. This indicates a rebellious soul with an inherent need to shock; who wants to be original rather than like everybody else.

Sun square Mercury: You may have been a shy child lacking in confidence or with a speech defect. The lesson of this square is to consciously use your creativity to communicate more effectively. If you do this, you can become a powerful speaker.

The T-Square

Following on from the square aspect, a *T-square* is a more powerful version of the square. It is formed when two or more planets are opposing each other and they square a third planet. In this formation, you have two squares present. Drawing a letter "T" in the zodiac is the easiest way to grasp this planetary formation.

The Grand Cross

Another aspect involving squares is the *grand cross*. This is formed when two pairs of planets are opposing each other. Think of a big plus sign dividing the zodiac into four. In this formation, you see four squares. The tension created by this rare aspect is strong and it will challenge you. If it can be harnessed effectively, it indicates great strength and success.

The Opposition

Relationship is the key to the meaning of this aspect and people with oppositions learn about themselves through interactions with others. Oriental astrologers relied on oppositions in arranged marriages believing opposites attract. However, this did not always make for a comfortable arrangement because with an opposition it feels like a perpetual tug-of-war! Like the square, the opposition is another of the hard aspects.

The key to an opposition is to bridge the divide because opposing energies are only apart until you have brought them together. You must use both planets in the opposition or one planet will predominate. While the square is urgent and demands action, an opposition is unsure and wavering. When you use your oppositions correctly, you are willing to consider the other side and can be an adept negotiator.

Venus opposition Saturn: You will be challenged by others until you realize how important you are. Stop underestimating your self-worth and don't give others more credit than they deserve. As your judgment sharpens, you become a skilled problem-solver. You are best working alone at your own pace because working with others arouses criticism. You can have romantic, loving relationships but there is generally some type of limitation or duty woven into your relationships.

This opposition is especially hard because it affects your love nature. There is a tendency to neglect the more difficult Saturn energies and live through the Venus. However, if you do that, Saturn will then appear to limit you in some way and may even ruin the relationship. If you live through the Saturn and ignore the Venus, you may end up alone in an ivory tower. With an opposition it's important to express both sides of the aspect in order to be happy and fulfilled.

Moon opposition Uranus: Donald Trump has emotional Moon opposing detached Uranus. In Trump's past there was upheaval and change and this has carried over as a restless emotional state. Trump fears being bored if he commits himself to a permanent relationship. Any long-term relationship he forms must have a lot of personal space and room to change and be spontaneous.

Aspects in Your Horoscope

Look at the aspects in your own horoscope. See if you have any planets making aspects to your Mercury. This speedy planet indicates the way you think and make connections, and aspects help to describe how you do this. If you have Saturn in aspect to Mercury, your mind will be serious and deep, prone to depression, fearful and cautious, as well as pragmatic and practical. You will have the ability to work hard and be disciplined. If you work hard you can excel as a speaker or writer.

Some other manifestations of this combination might be that your parents (authority figures = Saturn) were critical and perfectionist as you first began to talk. As a result you may have felt inadequate and slow to learn at school. This combination is actually one hallmark of folk who climb the ladder of success because of mental accomplishment, yet remain insecure about their intellect. I know two brilliant people with doctorates who both have Saturn in aspect to their Mercury, yet both lack real confidence in their intellectual abilities. This lack of confidence is a continual spur to further learning and success.

The deaf actress, Marlee Matlin, has Mercury making a difficult aspect to her natal Saturn. However, she used the power of this aspect to spur her to success. Albert Einstein had a similar aspect. He didn't speak until he was two years of age and was considered retarded when he entered school. His struggle to get his peers to accept his theory of relativity was long and hard-fought.

Astrologically-aware parents whose children have this combination might be concerned about language delays. As Saturn is associated with maturity and age, a child with this aspect will get better with age and become the eternal student.

What if you have a nice aspect from your Sun to lovely Venus? This would indicate a cheerful, charming character. You are good looking, attractive and popular, as well as a good listener and someone who enjoys people. The downside is that you attract people but don't know how to get rid of them. This is where a difficult aspect can help.

Now let's build the aspect picture a little more by also considering the houses the aspecting planets occupy. What if you have Mercury conjunct Saturn in your 6th House? How would you analyze that? First analyze your Mercury, then your Saturn. Having both in the house of health and work may indicate a person who is unable to work because of health issues, or on a positive note, one who teaches or communicates on health-related matters. In your 10th house, it would indicate a career involving communication, such as teaching or writing. As Saturn represents delays as well as success, this career may have been a long time coming with hard work associated with the success.

In this Step, we have looked at some examples of how the aspects manifest. Now look at each of the aspects in your own horoscope and analyze what they might mean according to the qualities of each planet involved, and the sign and houses they are in.

Step 4 Jargon

Aspects	The relationships planets make one with another. They are either harmonious (soft) or difficult (hard) in nature
Conjunctions	Planets that are 0 degrees, or next to each other
Sextiles	Planets that are 60 degrees (or two signs) apart
Squares	Planets that are 90 degrees (or three signs) apart
Trines	Planets that are 120 degrees (or four signs) apart
Oppositions	Planets that are opposite each other, or180 degrees apart
Orb of influence	A set number of degrees within which a specific aspect is effective

Stellium	When three or more planets are in conjunction
Grand Trine	When three planets, all in the same element, are approximately 120 degrees from each other
T-Square	When two or more planets are opposing each other and they square a third planet
Grand Cross	When two pairs of planets are opposing each other

Step 4 Exercises

- Learn the above jargon.
- List all the aspects you have with each of the planets in your horoscope.
- Note down if you have more soft or more hard aspects.
- Analyze the aspects to your Sun and Moon.
- Note the aspects to your Mercury and see if you can interpret how these affect the way you think and communicate.
- Note the aspects to your Venus and see if you can interpret how these affect your relationships.
- Note the aspects to your Saturn and see if you can interpret how these affect the way you work and your attitude to disciplines and authority figures.
- Note if you have any aspects to your North or South Nodes.
- Note if you have any of the more unusual aspects such as the Stellium or Grand Cross.

STEP 5

THE OVERVIEW: FROM JUDGMENT TO UNDERSTANDING

A horoscope is like the man it represents. It must be seen as a whole before any intelligent idea of its parts is possible. – Marc Edmund Jones

You have used your analytical left-brain skills by learning the jargon and completing the exercises. You have, hopefully, determined what Mars square Saturn means and learned why Venus in Sagittarius is different from Venus in Cancer. Now you can use your intuition. While the secrets of your horoscope won't be revealed overnight, you're now ready to take the leap from your lower, everyday, analytical mind (so prized by society) to your higher, intuitive mind; the stuff of vision, inspiration and genius.

Learning astrology is like playing a musical instrument. First you have to master the basics before your genius can be revealed. Despite the fact that I have been studying astrology for forty years, I still keep going back to the basics. The harder you work at these the more reliable your intuition will become. Learning astrology is definitely a *win-win* in which you not only learn about yourself but you can also improve yourself.

A common denominator of beginner astrology classes is that there's at least one student who knows absolutely nothing about the basics, yet who insists on asking seemingly profound, intellectual questions about some obscure piece of astrological minutiae. Instead of wanting to learn what Mars in Capricorn means she prefers to ask about an insignificant asteroid that will make no absolutely no difference to her life. This is an example of how our complexity-loving intellect can trick us into avoiding the hard work and discipline of learning the groundwork.

Spotting Themes

Now fire up your intuition by taking a long look at your horoscope; instead of analyzing the parts seek an overall impression. How does your horoscope look? Do you like what you see? Does it make you feel harmonious or uptight? In Step 1 you learned about the different patterns from *Splay* to *See-Saw*. Now let's look at the four quarters of your horoscope called the *quadrants*.

The Quadrants

As well as dividing your horoscope into twelve houses you can also divide it into four quarters comprising three houses each. These quarters are called *quadrants* and planets in the quadrants give yet another shade of meaning. Knowing about the quadrants adds to your overall first impression of your horoscope. The rule of thumb is to think about the qualities of the houses in each quadrant and then merge these qualities together.

The first quadrant comprises houses one, two and three. If you have more planets here you are (depending on other factors in your horoscope) assertive and self-oriented. This is a lifetime when you're learning about who you are and how you feel inside. You're getting in touch with what makes you feel comfortable and what gives you a sense of self-worth. It's a learning/teaching lifetime through interacting with other people.

The second quadrant comprises houses four, five and six. The majority of planets here indicate that your primary focus is on your personal life; your family, home, children and co-workers. You are learning how to interact with others. You are here to focus on your heart and personal creativity in ways that will bring joy to yourself and others.

The third quadrant comprises houses seven, eight and nine people. If you have most of your planets here you are learning about close relationships and how to become more diplomatic and socially adept. You are learning about cooperation, realizing that it's advantageous to honor other people's values and their different ideologies.

The fourth quadrant comprises houses ten, eleven and twelve and indicates an interest in politics, social causes and spirituality. You are likely to be independent, goal-oriented and original. You are able to see the "big picture" which allows you to more easily attain your aspirations. There is a longing for something higher than a purely personal life. In this lifetime you have chosen to adhere to causes that have a wider impact than just your own personal comfort and pleasure.

Missing Elements

In Step 1 we looked at how a person with missing planets in fire, earth, air or water signs can compensate by consciously attuning to the missing element. If, for example, you have no planets in earth, you can compensate by grounding yourself through exercise, massage or being more centered in the world of the physical senses.

Another compensating factor may be that this "no-earth" person has a very strong Saturn, the most grounded of the planets. If he has no planets in earth but Saturn conjuncts his Sun, he will have the practical ability of the earth element. So if you think you have a missing element in your horoscope, you now need to look and see whether this apparent lack is compensated by other factors.

Remember the houses are also connected to the elements. The 1st house is fire, the 2nd house earth, the 3rd house air, the 4th house water and so on around the zodiac. If you have no planets in fire but have a stellium of planets in your 1st house, for example, this would compensate for your lack of fire.

One client, Christopher, has no planets in earth but despite that appeared to be a solid, dependable and grounded person. This is because his Moon was in the 6th House, the *natural ruler* of which is the earth sign, Virgo. He also has a prominent, strongly-aspected Saturn conjunct his Midheaven. Remember, the Midheaven is like your banner and so Christopher seems disciplined and responsible. He is also self aware enough to compensate for this missing element and regularly practices Tai

Chi to ground himself. He also adheres to that four letter word, W-O-R-K, giving many hours of his time every week to volunteer work. However, the closer you get to this guy the more you also see his fiery, forthright, freedom-loving Aries Sun and Sagittarius Ascendant.

If you are a person with no planets in water you will have to deal with emotional, feeling issues more than most. You'll find that where there is a missing element, issues connected to that element keep appearing to be dealt with. I have clients with no water who spend an inordinate amount of time sorting out emotional problems. I suggest they add something watery to their daily routines such as swimming, keeping fish or taking long baths! When they do they invariably find that the emotional issues literally dissolve. It may seem strange but it is true.

If you have no or little air you feel blocked when trying to communicate or express yourself. I have a "no-air" client who is a college lecturer and sparkling dinner party guest. He admits that public speaking didn't come easily. He worked long and hard at it and by doing so brought this air element into his life. He does, however, have some trouble with his breathing, another potential problem with people lacking air. He now lives in as pollution-free a zone as you can get in the US and does regular aerobic exercise.

A close friend has no planets in fire. She's terrific, kind, clever and sharp-witted but can also be a damp squib, lacking initiative and a sense of adventure. She tells me she likes having me around because I perk her up, with my Aries Sun and Leo Ascendant. This is another thing you can do; surround yourself with people who have the elements you lack. You may feel a bit "out of your element" with them but it is definitely an interesting exercise. If you have little or no fire, be adventurous or live in the California sun! If you're not so lucky, get a real fireplace and sit in front of a roaring fire.

Strong planets-weak planets

Next take a look at your planets with a view to their strength. A *strong* planet is one that is prominently placed with many aspects from the other planets. You might think that because Venus in Libra is a peacemaker – eager to be liked and indecisive – that a person with this would be a pushover in relationships. However, if she also has powerful Pluto aspecting her Venus, she is more likely to be strong in her relationships, like the iron fist in a velvet glove. This is why it's important to consider all the aspects, not just one.

If you have what is called a *weak* planet or one with no aspects, it doesn't mean you are a weak person or one who won't amount to much. Astrology gives us the tools but it's still up to us whether we produce disaster or a masterpiece. President John F. Kennedy's Sun had virtually no aspects. This certainly didn't hold him back or stop him fulfilling his destiny. While not everyone with an unaspected Sun is going to be the President of the US, it shows what you can achieve if you set your mind to it. However, people with unaspected planets do often feel a sense of isolation. They may not ever mention it but you can bet that in some way they feel different or alienated.

I had a dear friend, an elderly lady with no aspects to her Moon. She told me that as a child she felt invisible. This was due to her overbearing English upbringing that demanded children should be "seen and not heard" which was one manifestation of her lonely Moon. One thing this invisible feeling can do, however, is push a person to want to be visible or to excel publicly. The lady made quite a name for herself in English upper crust circles by being outspoken on the subject of UFOs, a subject she cared passionately about. John F. Kennedy is another example of someone who pushed himself to become one of the most visible people in the world.

So, if you see what you think is a *weak* planet, look at the entire horoscope before passing judgment. You may be surprised to see an unaspected Mars in the horoscope of a football player. See if this is balanced out by something like planets in the Mars-ruled 1st house, or sign of Aries. In the same vein, if you have no oppositions in your horoscope it doesn't mean you won't be able to see another's point of view. This lack of an opposing viewpoint could be compensated by having planets in Libra or in the 7th House.

You are now beginning to see another layer of complexity in astrology where patterns emerge from your horoscope and repeat themselves as themes. After a while, these themes will bubble to the surface. The first time you know your intuition is working is when you actually start to feel the *person* behind the horoscope.

Double Whammies

You have realized by now that astrology is replete with rules and then exceptions to those rules. There is one rule to which you won't find any exceptions. This rules states that if you see a pattern once in a chart, it's a potential; if you see the same pattern twice, it's a possibility; but if you see it three times, it's a certainty.

My cousin, Carolyn, has mystic Pisces on her descendant, the cusp of her relationship house. Growing up, Carolyn drew poets, mystics and drop-outs alike into her life. She also has her planet of relationships, Venus, in the 12th house, the natural ruler of which is Pisces. On top of that, she has a third Piscean theme in that Neptune, the ruler of Pisces, was opposite her Venus. For years, Carolyn had a savior/martyr flavor to all her relationships. A repetitive theme that keeps popping up, refusing to be ignored, is called a *double whammy*. Eventually, Carolyn took to the religious life and ended up marrying an extremely devout English vicar. Carolyn is extremely happy and spends time working in soup kitchens and helping the poor and needy. She has interpreted this *double whammy* in her horoscope in a positive, compassionate way.

What Planet are You From?

One or more of the ten planets in your horoscope takes pride of place. These dominant planets are like keynotes. Since you choose your birth time and place (as well as your parents), keynote planets give clues about important issues. Read the synopses below to see if you think you're a *Solar* or a *Saturnian* type. This adds yet another layer to your interpretation.

The Solar Type

If you're a Solar type, you'll have a dominant Sun with lots of aspects. You may have a prominent Sun on one of your angles, the Sun or Moon in Leo, Leo Ascendant or planets in the 5th House. Whether or not you have shy Moon in Pisces or cautious Capricorn Sun, you could still be a Solar type. How do you recognize it? You are the budding monarch with a need to shine, to lead and be in the limelight. You are full of vitality and enthusiasm with a strong sense of self; you are the center of the universe who is born to rule.

The Lunar Type

I had a Scottish client with Sun in Libra and Pisces rising. With an initial glance at Andy's horoscope, you might have seen him as a poet, strolling soulfully by the lochs or basking in the heather, while writing about his bonnie wee lassie. The truth is that Andy was a very dour Scotsman. He is a predominantly Lunar type with a strong Cancer Moon in his chart and four planets, including Saturn in his 4th house of home and his roots.

The Mercurial Type

Perhaps you are chatty, full of nervous energy and never quite knowing when to stop. You are the Mercurial type with the Sun or Moon in Gemini, a Gemini Ascendant or planets in your 3rd house of communication. You may have Mercury on one of your angles with strong aspects. You are a natural born communicator. You can earn a living by selling ideas but can also squander time and energy on the phone and e-mail. You are curious, restless and witty, and brimming over with ideas.

The Venusian Type

With your strong Venus or Libran influence or planets in the 7th house, you may be a Venusian type; the God or Goddess of love. For you, relationships and love are keys to a fulfilling life. You are romantic, attractive and overly concerned with your hair and whether your shoes match your eyes. You are warm, considerate and caring with a hunger for appreciation and affection. Although a charmer, you can be overly concerned about what others think.

The Martial Type

Pugilistic by nature, you eschew a quiet life for a competitive one. You are the Martial type with a strong Mars, an Aries or Scorpio influence or planets in the 1st house. You are action-oriented and like to lead and achieve results. Geoffrey has Aries Ascendant, Aries Moon in Mars in his 1st house. He was hardly out of the cradle when he was shooting bows and arrows. He was a bundle of fun but hard work for his sweet Pisces parents. Martial types are competitive and aggressive and perhaps a little hotheaded with abundant vitality and energy. You are a good athlete or warrior, interested in the martial arts or the military.

The Jupiterean Type

You are the life and soul of the party; large in personality and with a tendency to be large of waistline. You like the good things of life. You drink, laugh, eat good food and generally enjoy yourself; not for you the strict diet or exercise routine. The French expression *joie de vivre* describes the Jupiterean type. You seek profound answers to big questions. You love to teach and preach to lesser mortals, which most of us are. On the downside, you can be inefficient and too easy-going to achieve anything much. You have a strong Sagittarian influence, such as the Moon in Sagittarius or Sagittarius rising, a strong Jupiter or prominent 9th House influence.

The Saturnian Type

Don't shy away from this one because although Saturnian types are serious, responsible, perfectionist workaholics they are just about the best friends. They are reliable, loyal, courteous and considerate. They can also be extremely witty with a dry, slightly caustic wit. How do you spot a Saturnian theme? Look at where Saturn is in your chart; is it prominent near an angle? Does it have several aspects? Do you have a Capricorn Sun, Moon or Ascendant or planets in your 10th house? Another piece of good news is that Saturnian types may be born old when their friends are still in diapers but as they mature they get younger and younger. They're not perfect but they're darn well trying.

The Uranian Type

You can spot a Uranian by their Mohawk hairdo and rings through every orifice. Uranus is the first of the outer planets and Uranian types are definitely unusual. People who are into astrology are often Uranian types (and believe me we astrologers are pretty odd...) as this planet rules astrology and the new sciences. These people dance to the beat of their own drum, which is a nice way of saying they are quirky, cranky and don't easily fit in. However, they also have a streak of genius so perhaps *we* should fit in with *them*. The Uranians have a strong 11th house, Aquarius Sun, Moon or Ascendant, as well as a strong Uranus. You know what to look for by now.

The Neptunian Type

There are similarities between Uranian and Neptunian types. Both are rather strange but in different ways. How do you know which predominates for you – Uranus or Neptune? I just have to ask you what time it is. If you look *at* your watch you're a Uranian. If you look *for* your watch you're a Neptunian. Neptune rules the mystic, the poet and the visionary, as well as the person who is confused and confusing. Unlike boundary-loving Saturn, Neptune rules the oceans, the ethers and the planes of inspiration. The Neptunian type is a person with one foot in this world and one in the next. There is usually an interest in things spiritual, creative and imaginary. Neptunian people with Neptune prominent, the sign of Pisces and 12th House highlighted, are hard to pin down. They seem to shape-shift from savior to saved, saint to sinner. More than most they need to immerse themselves in a spiritual, devotional life.

The Plutonian Type

Finally, there are the powerful Plutonians. They're all about power and psychic stuff with a prominent Pluto, Scorpio or 8th house. They are observers of people and life; mistrustful of themselves and others, which is a nice way of saying they are control freaks. Don't lie to a Plutonian type because they will see through you with their laser-like vision. My husband has a strong Pluto theme, with seven aspects to Pluto, Mars in the Pluto-ruled sign of Scorpio and Pluto in his 8th house. Gary has piercing, deep-set eyes typical of the Plutonian type. He is a healer of extraordinary power and can endure things that would melt a normal human and emerge transformed.

The Interpretation

After gaining an initial impression of the themes of your horoscope, you are ready to start your interpretation. Begin with the Sun, Moon and Ascendant, and see how these blend together. Look at your Moon sign to see what makes you feel warm and secure. First look at the sign and house your Moon is in, then analyze the aspects. By the time you have done this, you have a pretty good idea of how you react to things and why you feel as you do.

If you get to know your Moon, you will understand yourself a lot better. You will see if you are answering, or neglecting, your Moon's needs. You will understand your childhood and your emotional needs. If you're a man you will better understand your relationship with your mother and wife, as well as the feminine side of your nature. We need to understand our Moon's needs in order to feel happy.

Amanda has the Moon in Gemini in her 6th House. She needs to feel free to roam and dislikes being cooped up in an office as it affects her health adversely (in astrology, there's a relationship with work and health). It's anathema to Amanda to sit at a desk everyday never seeing or talking to anyone. She would be unhappy in this type of job because she needs to feel free not desk-bound. A better job for Amanda, depending upon other factors in her horoscope, would be as a teacher, sales person or dancer. It's important to understand your needs and cater to them or they will surface as problems. Keep your Moon happy but don't overindulge it.

Next analyze your Sun by sign, house and aspects. This is your character and what you are growing into. If your Moon is in reticent, shy Pisces and your Sun is in bold Aries, you may *feel* you just want to hide your head under the covers in bed and never emerge but you're learning about courage and leadership. If you want to grow, come out from under those covers!

Then look at your Ascendant and its aspects and analyze what this means. Your Ascendant is a filter and is also your mask. People with Leo rising do the mask thing to perfection because they are natural actors who want to show themselves in their best light at all times. Ask a person with Leo rising how they feel and they'll give you a sparkling smile and puff themselves up even if they're feeling lousy. They invariably look stunning even when crossing the Sahara desert by camel.

As an astrologer you've got to get behind the mask and understanding the Ascendant is the first step. A person with Aquarius rising may seem a bit quirky, aloof and defiant but is this hiding a reticent Cancer Moon? Ask yourself what is really going on.

Finally, look at your Moon, Sun and Ascendant together. Are they in the same or complementary elements? What about the modalities? Do you have a shy rising sign and an expressive Sun and Moon waiting to get out? Or is it that your exuberant Sagittarius Ascendant covers up for your modest Virgo Sun and secretive Scorpio Moon?

After you have analyzed your Sun, Moon and Ascendant, analyze the planets, starting with the nearest planet to the Sun, Mercury, and working outwards. Remember, Mercury is the way you think and your learning needs; Mars is the way you assert yourself and, if you're a woman, the type of men you're attracted to and your own masculine side.

This brings up an interesting point. The Sun in a woman's chart indicates the type of man she'll probably marry rather than the men she has previously dated, represented by Mars. Gina has her Sun in fun-loving Sagittarius and Mars in Scorpio and was attracted to dark and dangerous Scorpionic type men. Out of the blue a different type of man appeared in Gina's life; he was a typical openhearted adventurous Sagittarian and he was the one she finally married. Don't forget the Sun also indicates your Dad; it's not by chance that many of us women end up marrying men just like our fathers.

It's the same with Venus in a man's chart. A man with Venus in Aries will be attracted to sexy, alluring, bold women but if he has his Moon in home loving Cancer, he will prefer to marry the good cook! The woman he marries is nurturing and home-loving just like his Mom; probably very different from the assertive women he has dated.

Venus is also your relationships and the way you relate to others. Look at all the aspects it makes. Does it relate to Saturn? If so your relationships will be based on duty over love. What about Neptune? If Venus is in a dance with this planet you will be a hopeless romantic.

Jupiter indicates your luck factor. It describes talents and abilities acquired in past lives, and that's why it seems like luck but is actually your good karma working out. If you have Jupiter in your house of career you always seem lucky in finding great jobs. You do well with authority figures and probably will become one yourself. Power and authority sit easily on your shoulders and you use it wisely. The downside with Jupiter is that it is *laissez faire* – easy come, easy go. If you see Jupiter in the house of marriage, you may be looking at more than one. It doesn't have to be the case but one thing important to you in your relationships is growth, not security. You have this innate need to keep moving on in this area of your life. Also, unlike Saturn, Jupiter is not prepared to work at things.

Saturn tells you a lot about your integrity, maturity, sense of honor and character. If someone has a weak Saturn it usually indicates a certain immaturity. However, as mentioned previously, all weakness can be compensated by the character of the person concerned. Really get to know your Saturn sign because it's your Achilles heel. It will constantly trip you up until you learn to master it. Through hard work, it will become your greatest strength. Saturn *always* takes work. It won't just happen unless you make it happen.

William has Saturn in his 11th house of friends. He finds it difficult to make and maintain friendships and others regard him as distant and aloof. Because of this, his friendships are few and far between. However, he has a desire and need to develop deep, loyal friendships and feels lonely because they are not forthcoming. Nothing will change in William's life until he chooses to work at his friendships. If he does, he can have enduring friendships that will last a lifetime.

Uranus shows where you need to feel different, unique and special. I have it in my house of friends and I must admit I have unusual friends who are anything but dull. Wherever Uranus appears by sign and house is where you don't want anything ordinary.

Neptune shows where you are a mystic, romantic and otherworldly as well as forgetful. Remember that the outer planets affect a whole generation because they move so slowly through the signs of the zodiac, so you're looking at a generational influence. My generation had Neptune in Libra and we grew up in the 1960s and 1970s with Woodstock, hippies and free love. Now Neptune is in Aquarius, these babies will bring their humanity to earth in scientific ways, as a key for our future.

Pluto shows where you have the power to change. Look at the sign and house your Pluto is in as well as the aspects. Because of its extremely slow orbit it takes years to pass through the zodiac signs and so has a generational influence like the other outer planets but even more so. The house your Pluto is in signifies the area of your life where you experience power issues. If you have Pluto in your 1st house of personality, for example, you are probably an intense, controlling personality who likes to wear black and be noticed. In the 12th house you are marvelous at self-analysis but it is very difficult for you to open up to others. Finally, look at the Nodes of the Moon as indicators of destiny and the approach you should take to evolve and achieve your destiny.

Now you are ready to start the interpretation of your own horoscope. The following *Interpretation Guidelines* is a good place to begin. With your horoscope in front of you, answer each of the questions in these guidelines. Use the astrological glyphs, symbols and jargon instead of using regular sentences, to get used to writing the astrological language. Once you have answered these questions, you can then organize your notes into sections using the *Interpretation Outline* at the end of the Step.

Interpretation Guidelines

1. Look at the pattern of your horoscope. Is it a Splay, See-Saw, Bucket or Bowl?

2. Which element predominates? How many planets do you have in each element? Do you have a missing element or an over-abundance of one element?

3. What about the modalities? Are you predominantly cardinal, mutable or fixed?

4. What are the signs on the cusps of each house and what does this mean? Are some of your houses empty or full?

5. What about the four quadrants of your chart. Are the planets evenly spaced in each of them or bunched up together?

6. Do you have planets near the four angles, the Ascendant, descendant, MC and IC?

7. Now analyze your Sun, Moon and Ascendant. What houses are the

Sun and Moon in? What signs rules these houses. What is the sign on your Ascendant? Do your Sun and Moon have lots of aspects or very few. Are the aspects hard or soft?

8. Analyze the planets by sign, house and aspect.

9. Are the planets strong or weak? Do they have many aspects or are they in prominent positions.

10. Analyze your Moon's nodes by sign, house and aspects.

11. Now spot themes in your chart. Perhaps you have Capricorn rising and Saturn, the ruler of Capricorn, in your 10th house. This would be a double whammy.

12. What type are you? Solar or Saturnian, Venusian or Uranian?

Don't get bogged down with long interpretations at this initial stage but focus on a sketchy outline. Now group this information into sections as listed below. Under each section, briefly analyze the planets mentioned according to their sign, the house they are in and their aspects. Also analyze the houses by the sign on the cusp, number of planets in the house, etc. Finally, analyze the other points, such as the angles and astro-nomical points.

Interpretation Outline
1. Your Feeling Nature and Family Life
The Moon
Venus
4th house
The IC
2. Your Character and Leadership Potential
The Sun
Saturn
Mars
The Ascendant
1st house

The pattern of your horoscope

3. Your Mental Health and How You Learn

Mercury

Jupiter

3rd house

9th house

4. Your Relationships

The Moon

Venus

Mars

The Descendant

7th house

8th house

5. Your Career or Vocation

The Sun

Saturn

10th house

6th house

The Midheaven

6. Your Money and Values

Venus

2nd house

8th house

7. Your Creativity and Enjoyment

The Sun

Venus

Mars

5th house

8. Your Health

The Sun

Saturn

Ascendant

6th house

9. Your Ideals and Friendships

Uranus

11th house

10. Your Spirituality and Destiny

Neptune

Pluto

12th house

The Nodes of the Moon

You are now interpreting your horoscope and should begin to see definite themes emerging. The above *Interpretation Guidelines* and *Interpretation Outline* are not hard-and-fast rules to abide by but guides to get you started. After further practice and study you will expand your interpretation and in time evolve your own system. Whatever system you evolve, it's important to analyze all the planets, signs, houses, aspects and the other categories covered in this book.

What's most important is to remember your horoscope is about the real part of you with all your lessons, challenges and opportunities. It's not meant to be just an indicator of how lucky you are in love and how much money you can make. Although these things are important to all of us, they are not the main purpose of our existence. Some of the most important questions we can ask are: *"How can I learn and evolve?" "What can I give back to life and to the world?" "How can I make a difference?" "How can I give more love?" "How can I use my potential more fully?" "What is my destiny?"* Your horoscope can help you to see the answers and provide you with the necessary tools to unlock your potential.

The High Road or the Low Road?
No-one is created equal except for one aspect, the Divine Spark within us. Each of us is unique and at different stages of our journey through

evolution. If you decide to have an astrologer interpret your chart, I suggest you find one on a similar path to you or who is more aware than you are. If your astrologer is really into the basic "meat and potatoes" of life and you are on a spiritual quest, he's not going to be much help.

One of the challenges of all astrologers is whether a person is interpreting the beautiful energies of the planets in positive or negative ways. You probably won't know until you have a lot of experience and a developed, reliable intuition.

If you wish to become an astrologer, it's important to work on yourself as well as on your charts. Wisdom, discrimination and intuition are just as important as your technical skills because your words can affect people's lives. If you're not sure of something, it's better to give a positive interpretation than a negative one. If a person has Mars in Scorpio rather than telling him he is a sex maniac and control freak, speak of his intensity, passion and capacity for self-control. It may not be as specific but it's safer until you know for sure how he's handling his horoscope. Aim to be honest but also to inspire. Neptunian people can be saints or sinners; encourage them towards their sainthood. Don't plant seeds of doubt in a person's mind because they can take root and grow into nasty weeds. No planet is good or bad. Astrology teaches us how to find constructive uses of each planet, sign and aspect. In the symphony of the planets, we need every note.

May God bless and guide you in your cosmic journey through evolution, assisted and inspired by the advanced life forms of the stars and planets, living aspects of the Divine.

JARGON INDEX

South Node

Transits

Splash

Trines

Splay

T-Square

Squares

Uranus

Stellium

Venus

Sun sign

Water Sign